POCAHONTAS

TRUE PRINCESS

A YOUNG GIRL'S
BREATHTAKING STORY—
AND HER AMAZING JOURNEY TO
FAITH IN GOD

▲▲▲

POCAHONTAS
TRUE PRINCESS

▼▼▼

MARI HANES

MULTNOMAH BOOKS ◆ SISTERS, OREGON

Pocahontas: True Princess

published by Multnomah Books
a part of the Questar publishing family

© 1995 by Mari Dunagan Hanes
Illustrations © 1995 by David Danz

International Standard Book Number: 0-88070-873-5 (hd)

Cover illustration by Paul Bachem

Printed in the United States of America

For information:
Questar Publishers, Inc.
Post Office Box 1720
Sisters, Oregon 97759

Thanks be to God who has redeemed us
from every kindred and tongue,
from every tribe and nation.
REVELATION 5:9

Dedicated to the Hanes clan:
Cliff,
Sara Lace and Nora Grace,
Benjamin and Samuel

and to my Ancestors
who walked the "Trail of Tears"
while they sang *Amazing Grace*

CONTENTS

POCAHONTAS
TRUE PRINCESS

INTRODUCTION

FOUR HUNDRED YEARS AGO, in the area known as the Chesapeake (which means "Place of Many Shellfish"), there lived a courageous child whom we have come to know as Pocahontas. She was born into the Algonquin tribe of American Indians. During her childhood, people from England began coming to live in the Chesapeake, a land they called Virginia. They changed the life of Pocahontas and the world of the Algonquins forever.

Because many of the English wrote detailed letters and journals, we know a surprising amount about this child. In this fictional book I have tried to be true to history; the fictional parts of the story were added to tell true things about how an Algonquin princess might have lived and acted in the early 1600s.

The Walt Disney film *Pocahontas* sparked a great deal of renewed interest in this young girl, but her real story has even more adventure and courage and meaning than is often realized.

Many books have been written about the adventures of her short life, including her journeys to Jamestown and on to England. This book centers on her greatest journey of all — the journey of her spirit.

CHAPTER ONE

THE STOWAWAY

THEY WERE COMING! Although they wore moccasins and were treading along the riverbank as softly as deer, Pocahontas heard the rhythm of their steps.

She was hidden beneath a bearskin blanket in the bottom of a birchbark canoe belonging to the Brothers. She drew in her legs more tightly and rolled into the tiniest ball she could make.

They must not find me here, she thought. *I must go with them on this journey.*

Closer, closer they came. She heard no words exchanged. She knew no words were needed. There was complete under-standing between these two — Parahunt, her oldest full-brother, and her half-brother Tatacoope, the Fiery One.

She heard the sound of last-minute supplies being laid beside her in the canoe — the bow and arrows and spear, she guessed. The Brothers would keep those in easy reach.

She felt her hiding place begin to slide forward, scratching on the gravel beneath her ear as the canoe was pushed into the river.

She held her breath. The boat tilted and lowered as Parahunt took his usual place in front. Then came another swaying motion. That would be Tatacoope seating himself at the rear, closest to her hiding place.

Now, breaking his morning silence, the strong voice of Parahunt rang out. It was the prayer he always spoke with the first stroke of his paddle, as he lifted his face toward the sun.

"Thank you, Creator God," he chanted, "for the gift of Tree for this canoe, that we may ride upon the gift of your Great River."

The Brothers paddled in rhythm. The lap-lapping of water against the canoe was like a happy song to Pocahontas's ears. The water's delicious coolness pressed in through the birchbark. Joy rose in Pocahontas like a happy bubble that almost escaped in a giggle, but she tightened her lips. Her plan was working! She was going with them!

But where?

Pocahontas did not know.

She knew it was not to join other warriors on a hunt for the mighty whale. This was not the season. Besides, brave as she was, Pocahontas wasn't yet sure she wanted to ride on the sea waters which her people called Chesapeake, or farther out on the waves of the Great Gray Ocean. On the long whale hunts, the men of her village left behind their proud birchbarks like this. They went in bigger boats hollowed out from huge tree trunks, boats that held many strong arms paddling together.

In the nine summers of her short life Pocahontas had heard many stories about the whale hunts. Once an Older Brother was caught in the terrible thrashing of the whale's tail, and he never came home again.

Pocahontas also knew that Parahunt and Tatacoope were not

traveling to fight in a tribal war. Battles were much more common than whale hunts, for her father was the mighty Algonquin king who called himself Powhatan. He had conquered thirty tribes and now ruled over two hundred villages, so his people had known much fighting. But for many moons there had been no war dances in her village. Nor had she seen any war paint as the Brothers prepared for this journey.

It was clear that only Parahunt and Tatacoope had been chosen for the trip. From a distance she had watched them in secret counsel with their father. Their faces had been serious, their voices only whispers. She had watched them, too, as they tipped a spear with the shining metal that was bought at great price from a strange trader far to the north.

What could all this mean?

"Father, may I go with the Brothers?" she had asked.

Powhatan had raised his eyebrows and shaken his head in a firm No. There was not even a word of explanation. This had only increased her desire to not be left behind.

Soon the gentle motion of the canoe made her drowsy. Under the heavy bearskin, she felt as snug as a little squirrel nesting in a hollow tree. She slept. She dreamed of the Great River's beauty as she guided her canoe upon it. She rode through the shadowy green forest, until she reached the Chesapeake. There the Whale had come from the Great Gray Ocean to meet her and talk with her. Surely he would be friendly. Surely he would not thrash his tail at her.

Suddenly everything was shaking. She heard a crunching and a banging beside her head. With a frightened shriek she sat up and threw aside the bearskin blanket. Water splashed in her face. The world was white and wet and swirling.

The birchbark had just beaten its way through a stretch of rocky rapids. In an instant she feared nothing from the river, but plenty from the Brothers. The canoe slipped quickly into calmer water, but a storm was building on the faces of Parahunt and Tatacoope. They pulled in their paddles to drift in the slower current, as they scowled at the stowaway.

"Pocahontas!" Tatacoope shouted. He grabbed her ear and pulled until she cried. "You little trickster! You're as quick and sneaky and full of mischief as that little otter you keep! I think I'll go home and kill it for giving you his spirit!" He yanked her ear even harder.

"No!" she screamed, thinking more of her treasured pet than of her pain.

"Stop it!" Parahunt commanded. Tatacoope loosened his grip. But the fire of controlled anger she saw in Parahunt's eyes was even worse than Tatacoope's torment.

"You know Father told you not to come with us!" Parahunt spat the words at his sister. With a jerk of his arm he picked up his paddle.

"Yes, but I'm very brave!" she said, though more tears were forming in her eyes.

"I know," he answered.

"You're not going to war," Pocahontas stated. "I could see that."

"No," he acknowledged.

"And it isn't the season for hunting the mighty whale."

"No."

"Are you going to spy on our enemies, the Iroquois?"

"No."

"Then why can't I come?" she pleaded. She held up her little basket-purse filled with popcorn and dried berries. "Look! I've brought my own food. I won't be a burden."

Parahunt's mouth nearly curled into a smile, but she could see he was determined to be stern. "Food is not the problem, my little sister," he said simply. "We go on a journey which is man's work, not child's play. It's a journey you cannot understand."

"We can put her out right here," Tatacoope suggested. His tone was cruel.

Parahunt thought for a moment. "No, it's too far for her to walk alone in this time of mystery." Without saying more, he swung around the canoe, and began the strain of paddling upriver. They were going back to Comoco, the village of Chief Powhatan.

As she watched the strong arms of the Brothers fighting the current, Pocahontas sniffled with disappointment. *It isn't fair,* she thought. Why couldn't she be a part of this journey? After all, she herself helped build this canoe. She loved it as much as they did. She had helped round these inner braces by boiling branches in a clay pond filled with hot stones and water that she herself had carried. Parahunt even allowed her to sew some of the bark that had been carefully peeled in smooth slices from birch trees. With a bone needle her own fingers had pulled slender cords made from roots and elm bark to bind the birchbark slices together. Her own palms had rubbed in pine pitch for sealing the seams.

She remembered the grin on Parahunt's face: "My little sister has worked so hard," he remarked, "that she owns a part of this boat." Yes, she decided, she did.

The clear river rushed under the birchbark as she and the Brothers continued homeward. Pocahontas saw the sun's warming rays reaching all the way down to a school of trout. The forest on both sides was bursting with life. Beaver and mink were undisturbed by the canoe gliding silently by. She saw redheaded ducks and blue herons, and heard the geese honking overhead on their way north. In her peaceful delight she almost forgot she was going home, back to her girl-child chores, and back to her father.

Father will understand why I hid in the canoe, she told herself, grateful that she had at least come this far on the forbidden journey. Her father was very wise, for he had already lived nearly seventy summers. Yes, he would understand.

Or would he? She began to worry.

Too soon, a familiar sound announced their nearness to home. It was a waterfall in a stream that joined the river just above Comoco.

As they rounded a bend in the river, she could see the tall log fence Powhatan had built around the fifty wigwams of her village. The sight gave her a strange dread, a feeling it had never given her before. Dogs on the shore barked an alert.

Then she saw them. Powhatan already stood outside the log wall, and beside him was the Quiyow, the tribe's Spirit Man. The Quiyow's face was painted black, and he wore a cloak of weasel pelts and snakeskins. Something important was happening, or he would not have been there. He lived apart from the village, and Pocahontas had not seen him since the last ceremony of the Dark Worship. A knot of fear formed in her stomach. It always did whenever she saw him, though he had never spoken a word to her.

Besides these two, no one else was outside the wall.

The Brothers beached the canoe. As they helped her out, she

felt her knees trembling. Slowly she walked toward her father, staring at the ground. Her shoulders slumped.

"Daughter, look at me," her father commanded, when she stopped in front of him. His voice was like a cougar's growl.

She obeyed. She saw him towering above her. Fear and respect for Powhatan the mighty king came flooding into her heart.

He spoke slowly. "Your mother called you Matoaka — Little Playful One. I am he who named you Pocahontas — Favorite Daughter."

Pocahontas nodded only slightly, without smiling. There was no favor in her father's eyes today. His voice was empty of all kindness.

"I have loved you for your beauty," he continued. "I have loved you for your courage and your spirit. But your spirit must never again cross mine."

She swallowed, and quietly began to speak. "But, Father—"

"*Quiet!*" he commanded. "I have eighty-seven children. Not *one* of all the others would dare do what you have done today!"

She felt a tightness rise like a fist from her stomach to her throat, choking her. She turned away from her father's terrible gaze. The Quiyow's glare looked even more frightening. She lowered her head again. She saw the moccasined feet of the Brothers, who stood silently on either side of her.

"You must remember who you are," her father said. "You are Princess Pocahontas. One day you'll be a Spirit Woman, and you will rule over your own village. But today you've acted foolishly. You have worried and frightened your mother, Halewa, for she guessed at once what you had done and where you had gone.

"It has been decided that you will be given no food until the

Brothers return from their journey," Powhatan announced. "You will do only the tasks of the very youngest girl-children, for you have acted like a small child."

In her cheeks Pocahontas felt the burning of shame.

"This, too, will be your punishment," her father continued. She looked up. "No one may speak to you," he said, "and you may speak to no one — until the Brothers return."

Her mind was spinning with remorse and bewilderment. She saw Powhatan give a quick nod to Parahunt and Tatacoope. They hurried from her side. Behind her, for the second time this morning, she heard but did not see the launching of their canoe in the river.

Powhatan and the Spirit Man turned angrily and stalked back inside the wall to the village, leaving her alone.

Pocahontas began running. She ran past the wall and into the woods, then out on a grassy knoll overlooking the waterfall. This was her special place to think and be alone. She managed to get this far before falling to the ground and bursting into sobs.

Never before had she known such anger from her father. This was harsh medicine — bitter, bitter medicine.

CHAPTER TWO

PUNISHMENT

WHEN POCAHONTAS AWOKE at sunrise, her stomach already growled with hunger. She rose and put on her deerhide apron. This was her everyday clothing, as it was for all the children in the tribe.

She pushed open the wigwam's hide-covered door. Her mother was cooking her favorite breakfast: grilled trout and corncakes. Halewa looked up briefly from the stone-ringed cooking fire, but did not let her eyes meet those of her daughter.

Feeling like an outcast, Pocahontas walked silently past the cooking fire and down to her special place. There she knelt by the river to splash her face with tingling water.

Halfway across the stream, a shining, furry head popped up. The creature's sleek, silvery body rippled in her direction, then slipped out of the water and hustled to her side. He bumped his cold nose against her leg in loving recognition, and rolled onto his back.

She scratched his belly. "Good morning, Little Otter," she said, grateful for someone to talk to. "Today, you're the only one in the world who isn't mad at Pocahontas. And because of me,

Tatacoope is even mad at you. He's threatened to kill you. He says I've learned your ways. And maybe I have — I love you so much!"

This was the same spot where she had found her pet in the days of winter. He had been a tiny orphan, only as wide as her hand.

"Let him die," Tatacoope had said. "The otter cannot be tamed."

But Pocahontas came back often with chopped fish and even bits of deermeat to feed him. In only a few weeks he was filling himself with the crayfish that lived on the river's sandy bottom. He had never wandered far from her special place. He met her here each morning.

Little Otter jumped back into the water. She soon joined him there, but only for a short while. She knew it was time to face her punishment.

"Swim away, my friend," she called, as she stood on the bank to go. "Remember, we must both be careful!"

Back in the village, Pocahontas gathered firewood with girls who were only four or five summers old. All morning she kept wondering what adventures Parahunt and Tatacoope were having without her.

When the sun was highest, her mother came to her. She was carrying her sleeping baby, wrapped in soft rabbit skins. The boy had lived for four moons now, but had not yet been named. Halewa silently placed the baby in her daughter's arms.

Pocahontas took her brother inside the wigwam. She gently placed him in a cradleboard beside her mother's fur-covered sleeping mat. The other two mats in the wigwam belonged to Pocahontas and her older sister, Kahnessa.

The cradleboard's headrest was decorated with dangling sea shells. They reminded Pocahontas of the stories of her own babyhood. She, too, had rested in this cradleboard, and these shells were the first toys her tiny hands had played with.

She had been so small as an infant that her father was afraid to hold her. The Princess had been born too soon. Everyone thought she would die. When she survived and grew, her father called it a great sign — the sign of a child of great spirit. He began to love her.

"I knew then that you were set apart in beauty and spirit," he often told her. He said he soon noticed that she was the fastest of learners. Pocahontas had indeed realized long ago that her father and her brothers knew everything and understood everything, and she was eager to have them teach her. So many times she saw Powhatan watching with pride as she mastered the lessons of the forest and the river and the tides.

She especially remembered his approving smile as she brought him acorns she had dried and ground, or sugar harvested from maple trees, or the milky drink pressed out from walnuts.

She could always find sweet potatoes or wild artichokes before anyone else could. Bringing one of these to Powhatan was sure to make him wrap his arm around her and gladly call her name: "Pocahontas!"

Yes, she was his Favorite Daughter. Had she not been, how much worse his anger might have thundered yesterday when she returned in the canoe!

Pocahontas heard her unnamed brother stir from his sleep and begin crying. As she lifted the baby to rock him, she silently promised to find her father an artichoke as soon as she could.

It was the next afternoon before she could break away from

her chores and begin her search. Only water had entered her mouth in two days' time. Her stomach continued to complain, but this was not the worst of her punishment. Like all children in her village, she was taught to patiently endure hunger and pain.

But being silently ignored by everyone around her was something else. Talking with others always made Pocahontas feel their love for her. To not be able to talk was like not being loved.

Now she was glad to get away from everyone. At the edge of a marsh, under a covering of ferns, she found two tender arti-chokes. She wanted to fill her mouth with a bite of this delicacy. She saw ripe strawberries nearby, and they, too, tempted her. But she dared not give in. Her father's stern command had made all food taboo for her. She feared what harm the Spirit World would bring if she broke the taboo.

Pocahontas gathered the artichokes in her apron, and carried them back to the village. She entered her father's longhouse. No one was there. She left her peace offering in a serving basket next to his council chair. He would know whose gift they were.

The next morning Halewa motioned for her daughter to fol-low. Pocahontas stepped along happily, for her mother was chanting the Planting Song. This was another planting day for corn and beans, and Pocahontas always enjoyed working in the fields.

When they got there, Pocahontas was allowed to do only what younger girls did: dropping four grains of corn and two beans into every seed hole. The holes were being carefully made — just the right depth, just the right distance apart — by the women and older girls. Halewa and the other women gossiped as they worked. Her sister Kahnessa and the other girls laughed and told stories. Pocahontas stayed silent.

Well before the sun was at its highest, a call rang out from the village.

"Parahunt has returned!"

At once, Pocahontas glanced at her mother. Halewa smiled. "The punishment is finished," she said. She took a corncake from her pocket. "Here, my Matoaka. Eat."

"May I go see them?" Pocahontas hurriedly asked.

"Yes, my child."

Corncake had never tasted so sweet, but Pocahontas swallowed it on the run.

The Brothers were just stepping out of the canoe when she reached the riverbank. She hurried close.

Tatacoope saw her first. He frowned, and spat, and called her "Little Otter" under his breath. Parahunt caught her eye and smiled. He reached out to ruffle her hair.

Chief Powhatan came through the gate in the log wall, with the gruesome old Quiyow at his side, as well as several warriors. Her father did not seem to notice Pocahontas. She wondered if he had found the artichokes.

Parahunt stopped solemnly in front of the men. He began his report at once, as more villagers continued to gather around.

"It is true, Father! I have seen it with my own eyes. Three great ships with sails as big as clouds have landed at the mouth of the Chesapeake. White men have come to the land of Powhatan!"

Pocahontas heard several villagers gasp and murmur. They all knew stories of the bearded white foreigners who had visited other tribes. Even her own grandfather, Powhatan's father, had fought with these strangers called the Spaniards, far to the south. But now they were here!

Parahunt's words were clear and slow: "We hid close by, as you told us — seeing all, but never being seen. We counted one hundred and four fair-skinned soldiers wearing breastpieces and hats of metal. They have many weapons."

Pocahontas saw her father's face darken.

"We must watch them," he commanded. "We must watch night and day. Watch, and wait."

Pocahontas gazed back and forth from her father to her brothers. She was alarmed by what she saw. Their faces were tense. They were puzzled. Was it possible this was something that they did not know? Was this something strange that they did not understand?

CHAPTER THREE

CARTWHEELS

ONE LATE-SUMMER MORNING, Pocahontas awoke to hear her mother singing another familiar chant.

For as long as she could remember, the seasons and days had been marked and measured by song. There were planting songs and harvest songs. There were songs for clamming and songs for fishing. There were songs for the dying, and songs for new birth. There were songs of war and songs of peace.

Today's song was her favorite. Mother was humming the Berry-picking Song, which meant that today was Celebration Day.

"It's here!" Pocahontas shouted. "And this time I get to wear a grown-up dress!"

Halewa laughed. She had laid out the new dress on her sleeping mat. "Yes," she said. "It's ready."

Pocahontas feasted her eyes on every part of it. It was a royal dress, made of bleached white buckskin that her mother had soaked and stretched and scraped with an elkhorn. The edges of the sleeves and skirt were striped in red and yellow paint that Halewa prepared from roots. Across the front and arms were tinkling rows of tiny, round cowrie shells. There was even a buckskin cap that matched.

Pocahontas reached out to finger the shells.

"But first," her mother said, "you must bathe and finish your morning work."

Pocahontas was out of the wigwam in a flash.

She went as usual to the river, where most of the other village children were enjoying their daily bath as well. There were mornings in the winter when holes had to be cut in the ice so the children could jump in for a few shivering moments. But on hot summer mornings like this, being in the river was pure delight.

Pocahontas dove in. Under water, she watched for Little Otter. From the hazy, blue-green distance he came, leaving a stream of bubbles in his wake. He zipped around her in a circle before they both rose to the surface for air.

"Good morning, Little Otter!" she sputtered. "Happy Celebration Day!"

The other children joined in: "Happy Celebration Day, Little Otter!" They enjoyed her pet as well, but he would allow only Pocahontas to touch him, and only she had known the brush of his velvety body against hers.

Usually the summer mornings were times for races and other swimming competition. But today the children quickly put their simple animal-hide aprons back on. Pocahontas, too, hurried away to finish her morning chores.

The first chore was to check the Brothers' fish traps. They were in a cool, green pool upriver from the village. They were woven from willow branches, and had doors made of sharpened twigs that closed when a fish had gone inside.

These basket traps were always a wonder to Pocahontas. When she was younger she had been fascinated to watch Nantoda, the village's old basket-weaver, as she worked all winter to make new ones.

"I can make my own trap," little Pocahontas had announced one day to Nantoda.

"Really?" the old grandmother responded. She explained that it had taken many years for their ancestors to learn the best way to trap fish. But Pocahontas was confident she could do it faster. She spent days twisting branches and tying reeds together, but a jumbled mess was all she made. How Nantoda laughed!

Then Pocahontas had a different idea. She borrowed one of her mother's grain baskets and added a few sharp sticks around the rim. She placed it in the river beside the traps of the Brothers. Day after day that spring, she lay on the riverbank as still as a log, watching the clear water. Fish after fish swam into her basket. And fish after fish swam out, only to enter the Brothers' traps and be caught. Finally even a princess had to admit defeat. She learned that some things cannot be done with shortcuts, and the Old Way is very often the best.

Of course, she was only a little girl then. Now she was a big girl, with a big girl's buckskin dress.

On this Celebration Day, the beginning of berry-gathering, the Creator God was already smiling on her. Two of the basket traps held big shining trout! Pocahontas scooped up the traps and carried the treasure on a pole, back toward Mother and the breakfast fire.

As she walked, she wondered about the strange tribe of pale men living somewhere down the river. It had been four moons since she had stowed away in the canoe. The village had seen nothing of the white men since the Brothers reported their arrival, but the spies Powhatan sent out had much to tell. They said the great sailing ships had gone away, and the strangers who remained had built shelters behind a great wall. They said the pale men were trying to hunt and fish, but their ways did not seem wise.

No matter what these white men tried, Pocahontas thought, they would never be as good at catching fish as the traps of the Brothers.

Back in her wigwam, Pocahontas slipped into her dress. Again and again she murmured her thank you to her mother: "La-tee-nah! La-tee-nah!"

"It's a little big," Halewa said, "but you'll grow like a corn-stalk after the rain."

Pocahontas watched her sister dress for the celebration as well. As Kahnessa picked up a berry-picking basket and stepped through the door, she smiled and whispered to Pocahontas: "Finally, Remcoe and I can spend a day together." Pocahontas thought Remcoe was a kind and handsome brave. She was glad he wanted to marry Kahnessa.

All the village maidens were dressed in their finest, and stood beside their wigwams, holding their baskets. It was the custom on this day for a young man to stroll by the wigwam of the maiden he most admired. If she favored him, she would allow him to carry her basket and walk with her to gather berries.

Remcoe approached Kahnessa and opened his mouth to speak. But no words came. He swallowed hard, and looked pleadingly at her. Kahnessa smiled at his wordless question, and the two walked away together.

"Why can't Remcoe ever talk to Kahnessa?" Pocahontas asked her mother. "He always has plenty to say to everyone else."

Mother laughed. "Oh, that is often the way of a warrior with his maiden. One day Remcoe will find the right words."

Halewa carried her Boy-with-no-name as she and Pocahontas made their way to the center of the village, where everyone was gathering around the chief. The cowrie shells on the Princess's dress filled the air with a clattering rhythm. "You'll make music wherever you go," Powhatan said when he saw her. "The Song of Pocahontas!"

Remcoe was bringing out gifts to shower on the family he hoped to become a part of. To Chief Powhatan he gave fishhooks made from eagle bones and talons. To Halewa he gave the treasure of red feathers from the cardinal. He even remembered Pocahontas with a new necklace strung with roanoke shells.

There would be many berry-picking days ahead for all the women and children. But on this first day, the Celebration Day, everyone marched out together. In front were Father and his family. Unlike most of the tribe, Father had many wives, so his clan made a lengthy parade.

When the slow-moving procession finally reached the Celebration Meadow, a signal was given. At once the children raced free-for-all to the berry patch to find the best branches. Pocahontas was small for her age, but she ran like the wind, as fast as many boys. There was good-natured scuffling as she claimed a bush loaded with ripe berries, and quickly began filling her basket. Remcoe and Kahnessa soon joined her. Her girlfriends Nanoon and Kewelah were right beside her as well, laughing and teasing and gathering the ripe fruit.

Pocahontas was tempted to plop a berry into her mouth, but

she and all the children knew the rule. No berries could be eaten until the tribe returned to the village that evening and danced with the baskets in a Circle of Thanksgiving to the Creator.

Suddenly, on this happy day, Pocahontas was saddened with memories of last year's Celebration Day. Lominas had gathered berries with her then — Lominas her cousin, Lominas her childhood friend and constant companion, Lominas-who-was-no-more.

He had stood right here beside her, making her laugh with his silly looks and his teasing and his own funny version of the Gathering Song. The force of his happy life came leaping into her mind. Her sorrow for her cousin was stronger than her fear of the Spirit Man's taboo.

"Oh, Kahnessa," she barely whispered, so no one else would hear. "I miss Lominas."

"Hush, Pocahontas!" Kahnessa warned. "You know the mention of his name is forbidden. Hush!"

Pocahontas pressed her lips together, as her sister continued: "You'll be a Spirit Woman yourself one day. It's already decided. You must make yourself understand the taboos. And the Dark Worship, too."

Pocahontas again felt the knot of fear in her stomach.

"Besides," Kahnessa added, "what is done, is done."

Pocahontas went on picking berries, staining her fingers blue. She said no more about Lominas, but his memory stayed with her. She had known him so well. How could she ever dishonor him by forgetting him completely?

When all the baskets were full, the gatherers were rewarded for saving every berry: The best of all foods had been brought to the Celebration. There was freshly smoked salmon, and corncakes sweetened with honey. There were baked birds and sweet potatoes and popcorn.

After the feasting came the games, in which all but the very old and the very young took part. A toothless grandmother watched Boy-with-no-name so Pocahontas and Halewa were free to join in. They were on the same side in double-ball. Everyone on both teams carried sticks. They used them to carry or toss the double-ball, which was two rounded stones tied together with a leather thong. The action went back and forth toward the goals at each end of the field. Pocahontas was glad to see Halewa still as swift and agile as her daughters.

Only the women and girls played double-ball, while the men saved their energy for the brutal game of lacrosse. After the men took the field, the air was filled with screaming, taunting, and groaning. Pocahontas soon saw Tatacoope rubbing a knot on his head as big as a goose egg.

As the humid afternoon grew hotter, Pocahontas was steaming in her buckskin dress. She nodded to Nanoon and Kewelah. The three of them slipped away from the crowded meadow. They ran through the cool of the forest until they reached a place where Pocahontas took off her royal dress, leaving on only the apron-dress she wore underneath it. She carefully hung the buckskin dress on a tree branch with her cap. "I'll be grown up soon enough," she said to Nanoon. "I've spent enough time today dressed as royalty."

Then the girls were off for adventure, running like the bounding deer they knew so well. They skipped down hills and splashed through creeks. They frightened creatures who were accustomed to shaded silence.

The children began a game of Hide-from-the-Hunter.

Pocahontas was the deer. While the eyes of the "hunters" were hidden, she slipped away silently. Further and further into the forest she crept, keeping her weight on her toes, just as Parahunt had taught her.

She stepped out of the woods at the top of a grassy hill. She sat and listened for a long while. There was no sound of her friends. They hadn't been able to follow her. She was winning the game!

She continued her silent waiting at the top of the green slope. Then she could no longer withstand the challenge of this perfect play-hill. Pocahontas threw herself down, rolling over and over, all the way to the bottom. There she jumped up and practiced her favorite move — four cartwheels in a row.

She paused to clear her head. But she was so happy she couldn't stay still. It was Berry-picking Time, and she had escaped the hunters, and she was Princess Pocahontas! She threw herself into more cartwheels.

A branch crackled, and the Princess looked up with a start.

What she saw was terrible, and a shiver went through her body.

On top of the hill stood not a wild animal or even an enemy Iroquois, but a tall and very pale being. His yellow hair blew in the breeze. His face was covered with hair like fur. He was wearing more clothes than the Brothers would wear even in winter. And his eyes were the same color as the sky!

He stared down at Pocahontas. She was frozen with fright, unable to move or even breathe.

This must be one of the white soldiers! Would he kill her? Would he eat her? Who could guess what a stranger such as this was thinking?

Suddenly the creature's face broke into a wide grin. His blue eyes twinkled, and he laughed aloud.

Why was he laughing? It reminded her of what her own father or brothers might do if they had been watching her cartwheels.

Then the stranger did what was unthinkable. He dropped down on his side to lay in the grass, and rolled down the hill like a child, exactly as she had done. He must have seen her!

He came to a stop only a few paces from Pocahontas. He stood, brushed his clothes with his hands, and grinned at her again.

Slowly, shyly, she found herself smiling back at the white man.

Her legs were shaking, she suddenly realized. The Princess gathered her thoughts. She must go. She forced herself to turn away and run toward the woods.

At the edge of the trees she turned. The bearded man was still smiling. Pocahontas raised her hands in simple sign language: "I am a friend." Would the pale stranger understand?

Her feet pounded a steady rhythm back, back to find her friends and her dress, back to the safety of her people.

As she ran, she decided not to speak of what she had seen. Her father might be even more angry than when she hid in the canoe. No, she would tell no one. This would be her secret. She might have met great danger at the enemy's hands. Instead she found the gift of laughter.

Who was this stranger, this Yellow Hair? He must be brave, to wander through the forest and leave the other soldiers behind.

Would her eyes ever see him again?

CHAPTER FOUR

WINTER FIRES

THE SNOW WAS MELTING in a wide band around the growing
fire. Pocahontas threw more branches on the roaring blaze, then
stepped back from the heat.

She was still holding on to one stick. She pointed with it.
"Right there, Nanoon," she said to her friend. "Put some there."

Nanoon reached behind her to a pile of cold, blackened
stones. She gathered three of them in the crook of her left arm,
and stepped toward the fire. With an underhanded swing, she
aimed for the spot Pocahontas was pointing to. One by one,
each stone hit the mark, landing with a plop in the raging red
coals.

Pocahontas looked up. Today the smoke rising overhead was
the same color as the wooded mountain tops she saw in every
direction. Just yesterday her people had arrived at their winter
hunting camp here in the Blue Haze Mountains. Algonquins
from other villages had come as well. Only the very old and the
very young had stayed behind.

Before sunrise tomorrow, more than a hundred men from

these villages would go out together on the first daily hunt. To get them ready, everyone had work to do today.

"More stones, Nanoon. Right here." Pocahontas was pointing her stick again. Nanoon was two summers younger than Pocahontas, and Pocahontas was teaching her the job of tending the fire for the steam-bath stones. Only twenty paces from the fire was the bark-covered sweathouse. Fire-hot stones were dropped on the floor of this large hut, with water poured over them. Several sweating braves were sitting in the hot steam inside. Later they would run from the sweathouse to jump in a snowbank or into the creek that ran through the hunting camp. Then they would soak in water filled with ferns to give their bodies a woodsy odor for the hunt.

Pocahontas thought the fire seemed big enough and hot enough, and there were plenty of stones heating up. She stepped back from the blaze toward the sweathouse, while Nanoon went to gather more branches for the fire.

From inside she heard a gruff voice she didn't recognize. It must be a warrior from another village. Pocahontas stopped breathing when she heard what he was talking about. She stepped closer.

"The pale men had a hard summer. Now they're having a worse winter. They're sick and hungry. They told us they want to trade for corn."

The next voice she heard was Tatacoope's: "Maybe it's time to attack them again, as soon as the hunt is over. Perhaps many of us should go this time, and not just you warriors from Paspeg."

"No," said the first voice. "They still carry the thunder-sticks, and they'll use them again, just as they did to kill some of us. They also have the giant thunder-sticks guarding their village. But they're already as weak as children. They were foolish in the first place to build their village in that lowland. The swamp fever and the ocean storms will destroy them. We don't need to. We can wait."

The men were quiet. A chill came over Pocahontas. She stomped her feet and returned to the fire. She wondered if Yellow Hair was still alive, after all these moons since she saw him rolling down the hill.

When darkness came that night, Pocahontas and Nanoon were seated not far from another fire that crackled in the middle of the hunting camp's longhouse. The girls were wrapped together in a bearskin. They were squeezed into a room filled with people. The air was hazy with smoke from the fire and from several glowing tobacco pipes.

Two drummers beyond the firepit had already begun a steady pounding rhythm. Behind the drummers, Chief Powhatan sat on a mountain of furs, surrounded by most of his wives. But Halewa was not with him. Instead, Pocahontas saw her mother standing near the door at the far end of the longhouse. In the dim light, Pocahontas could not see what expression Halewa's face wore.

Just then, through the door, the Quiyow entered. The packed crowd made way for him as he stepped across the room. He took his place beside the chief, and stared ahead as if in a trance. Pocahontas wondered if there was some Dark Magic he wanted to perform tonight. She gladly turned away from him to look at old Macomba, who had just seated himself before the fire to begin this night of storytelling. Macomba was her people's favorite storyteller.

The drums continued their throbbing as Macomba's voice began to chant. Around the room, several rattles joined in the rhythm.

Macomba first praised the mighty Chief Powhatan. He told of the battles in which the king led his warriors to victory.

He made the Algonquins into one. He brought them together by his mighty rule. Village after village he conquered...

The song went on to name each tribe and village that Powhatan had overcome. Pocahontas knew the story well, but always enjoyed it again. She leaned forward to catch every word. When the Conquering Song was over, everyone yelped with approval as Chief Powhatan looked on proudly.

Macomba's next tale was the Story of the Earth. He told of the days when mountains breathed fire and smoke. He spoke of how people once hunted creatures far bigger and more fierce than any hunted now. He sang about the Far Land where the people once roamed. He talked about the Great Flood that killed men and beasts, and marked the land forever.

Pocahontas tugged the bearskin more tightly around her shoulders. She felt as if she were a part of that ancient world. She wanted to journey there tonight in her dreams.

Next Macomba told a favorite tale that made Pocahontas and Nanoon giggle. It was about a silly squirrel who worked hard to store up nuts, then forgot where he hid them. It was the kind of story that could go on and on, and Pocahontas hoped it would. But the chant faded away too soon. The Quiyow had come forward to stand in front of the fire. Macomba moved aside.

Pocahontas thought the Spirit Man looked older than old. His wrinkled face did not remind her of the ancient world, like Macomba's face did. The Quiyow's oldness was dark and dreadful.

The firelight was dimmer now. The drums sounded to a slower tempo.

The Quiyow closed his eyes. He leaned back his head and opened his mouth. Out of it came a high-pitched wail that hurt Pocahontas's ears.

Unlike Macomba, who sat still as he chanted, the Quiyow swayed from side to side. Above his head he shook a hollow club with rattling pebbles inside.

The Quiyow reminded everyone that Ahone the Creator God had made the world, and Ahone was good. But now Okewas the War God ruled the world, and he was terrible and bad-tempered. Everyone must please Okewas, he chanted. The War God was powerful. Okewas must be carefully obeyed. Okewas must be carefully worshiped. The War God must be followed into battle. The War God must have the sacrifices he demands.

Beneath the bearskin, Pocahontas noticed that Nanoon was trembling. Pocahontas as well could not hold back a shudder.

She looked across the room. Halewa was stepping out the doorway.

When the Quiyow finished, Pocahontas slipped out from under the bearskin and made her way across the crowded room. As she stepped out the door, she heard Macomba beginning the Song of Remembrance to honor the warriors who died fighting against the Iroquois and the mighty Huron.

Outside, Pocahontas saw her mother on the snow-covered slope above the longhouse. She walked closer. Halewa was looking at the stars. Pocahontas saw tears in her eyes. She put her arm around her mother's waist. She knew Halewa was thinking about her sons who had been killed in battle. Silently they listened to the Song of Remembrance coming from the longhouse below.

Finally Mother spoke. "Our War God is not a god who cares about the hearts of women," she whispered. "The worship of him is a painful and empty worship."

Pocahontas thought at once of Lominas, and the sacrifices that Okewas demanded in the Dark Worship. Halewa must be thinking about this, too. But surely her mother would never dare to speak about it.

Pocahontas locked both arms around her mother. For a long while they watched the stars together.

Then they walked hand-in-hand across the crusted snow to their sleeping hut. "Do not dream tonight of the Dark Magic," Halewa said. "Dream instead of old Macomba's stories."

"Yes, Mother, I will," Pocahontas promised.

CHAPTER FIVE

THE PRISONER

EARLY ON THE FIRST morning after her people's return from the hunting camp, Pocahontas was bringing back several trout from the basket traps. Lying on the trail to Comoco was a long white feather. She stopped at once to pick it up. "White Feather" was her secret name, her spirit name. She gave thanks to the Creator God for the feather, and wondered what special purpose it might serve.

As she came nearer to the village, she saw a tight ring of children gathered around the ceremonial staff at the center of the village. Some were jumping up and down. She hurried to see what they were looking at.

She was alarmed when she got closer. Seated in the center of all the attention was the Quiyow. He was threading a live garter snake through the large hole in his left ear lobe. He pinned eagle bones through the snake's body on either side of his ear to hold the wriggling creature in place.

He reached in a pouch at his side and pulled out another snake. This one he threaded in his right ear.

Pocahontas knew these serpent earrings could mean only

one thing: The Spirit Man was calling on his most powerful magic. No doubt he was preparing to challenge someone.

Pocahontas told herself that she should not turn away from what the Quiyow did. After all, she herself would be a Spirit Woman someday. She prayed for the Creator God to make her more spiritual.

Behind the gathering, Pocahontas saw Tatacoope rushing by. She ran to him. "What is happening?" she asked.

He stopped and thrust out his chin and lower lip in a way that told her he had important information, and was proud of it. "They're bringing him here," he said. "Tonight!"

"Bringing *who* here?"

"Who? Why, the white soldier who's been captured."

She knew the look on her face told Tatacoope how desperately she wanted to hear more. She also knew how satisfied he was to leave her in suspense. Before he hurried on, he raised his eyebrows and added, "And around the prisoner's neck he wears a floating arrow. It's powerful magic!" That was all the news he would share. He was off to the council longhouse.

Tatacoope would have nothing to do with her the rest of the day. Even Parahunt shrugged off her questions. But by sunset she had snatched up rumors from a few women: The prisoner was a white chief. He and six other pale strangers had wandered into the land of the Pamunkey people, but the Pamunkeys had killed or chased away the other six. The white chief had a thunder-stick, and he killed three warriors before he was captured. The Pamunkeys had taken him to her father's brother, Chief Opech of the Paspeg people. And Chief Opech himself was bringing the prisoner here.

As the sky darkened, the booming rhythm of the tom-tom

drums announced the meeting in the council longhouse. All the most important members of the tribe were being summoned. Pocahontas quickly dressed in her regal white buckskin. Over it she put on a cape of white feathers flowing from her shoulders to her moccasins. She was young for such a gathering, but as Chief Powhatan's favorite daughter, she was able to enter the longhouse without a challenge from the grim-faced brave guarding the door.

She walked forward in the smoky room, mostly unnoticed by the murmuring crowd inside. She thought the painted warriors standing in rows must number more than two hundred. There was also a row of stately women wearing long feather capes like her own. She found a place to stand between Mother Halewa and Opposso, her father's sister, who ruled her own village at Appamatucks.

Only Chief Powhatan was seated. His throne near the firepit was a log platform covered with raccoon and fox furs, with the tails hanging down. He wore an eagle-feather crown. His favorite wives stood closest to him, all wearing their finest beadwork and pearls. Parahunt and Tatacoope were also nearby.

The drumming stopped. Everyone watched in silence as Chief Opech of the Paspegs strode into the room, with the captured white man behind him, guarded by warriors.

Pocahontas gasped as she saw the prisoner's face. Instantly she recognized his yellow beard and hair. And even here, inside a room at night, his eyes were the color of the noonday sky.

He was brought near the throne. Pocahontas thought he showed calmness and courage as he looked up at her father.

Chief Powhatan nodded, and everyone sat down. Opposso stepped forward and offered Yellow Hair a bowl of water for washing, and feathers for a towel. There would first be a feast of deer and pheasant and turkey. Every guest must be fed, whether friend or enemy.

Pocahontas noticed that Yellow Hair seemed too weary to take even a bite. She herself could hardly swallow. She could not pull her eyes away from the white chief's face. She saw something round and made of metal hanging on a string around his neck.

When the meal was over, the prisoner was pulled to his feet. The drums began beating. From the shadows at one end of the longhouse, Pocahontas heard the wailing chant of the Quiyow. He made his way forward until he was dancing around the captive. He wore a headdress of rattlesnakes and stuffed weasels. The weasel tails were tied together and stood up in a waving mass on top of his head. The struggling garter snakes were still in his ears. He was shaking his rattle-club above his head.

As the Quiyow danced, he threw handfuls of ground cornmeal and powdered tobacco to sizzle in the firepit.

His wailing ended and the drums pounded to a loud, final blast. The Quiyow stepped to the side of Powhatan's throne, and stood there.

Chief Opech stepped forward. Pocahontas saw him looking at the Quiyow before he addressed Powhatan the king. "This white man was caught trespassing on Pamunkey land," he said. "He hunted there without permission. With his thunder-stick, he killed three of our brothers, the Pamunkeys.

"It is true that he wears the magic arrow that floats in a circle. But the magic is not strong. I have watched this man. He gets tired, like any of us. He gets hungry. He bleeds. So I say, we shall kill this white chief, as a sign to all the other white men who have come."

The room erupted with whoops from the warriors. But the shouting finally died down when the white chief held up his hands. He wanted to speak. Pocahontas thought this was useless, for she had heard today that the strangers spoke a blabbering language that could not be understood.

"Chief Powhatan, my name is John Smith." Pocahontas was amazed. His words were in the Algonquin tongue.

"I know you're a mighty chief," he said. His words were halting and awkward, but Pocahontas clearly understood him. "I have traveled in many far lands. I have visited many tribes of people. I have never seen any tribe so great and so wise as the people of King Powhatan. That is why I have learned your words.

"But when I went hunting, I could not know on whose land I was walking. I came to hunt for deer. Our people are hungry. They are not as good as your people at catching fish."

This comment brought chuckles and the nodding of many heads.

"It is true," he went on, "that I took the lives of three Pamunkey men with my thunder-stick. But it was only after they had killed my men. I do *not* want war with the mighty people of Chief Powhatan. I want to trade with you."

He cupped his hands around the metal disk that hung on his neck, and held it forward. "In my village," he said, "I have many wonderful things like this floating arrow to trade with the chief. I have copper. I have many beads. I only want to trade."

Pocahontas stared at the white chief's face. She was certain now that this John-Smith was not an evil man. Surely her father would see this.

But the Quiyow gave a violent shake of his rattle-club, and let out a frightening wail. "The white chief must die!" he cried. "For the honor of Okewas! This is what the War God wants!"

The warriors whooped again. Once more the Quiyow leaped in front of the throne to dance around the prisoner. The drums began booming. Faster and faster the Spirit Man whirled, until he finished with a soul-piercing scream.

The warriors kept shouting and shaking their fists. Everyone in the room was standing now. Chief Opech and two braves rolled a round granite stone from a corner of the room, and let it fall in front of the throne. Then other warriors surrounded the white chief and dragged him to the stone. Tatacoope was leading the way.

Pocahontas had seen this before. She groaned at what she knew was to follow. She wanted to cry, she wanted to scream, but in the noisy madness of the room she knew it would not help.

Tatacoope's arms pressed against the prisoner's shoulders, forcing his head on the stone. The other warriors raised their clubs.

Pocahontas could stand it no longer. Without thinking, without a warning, she rushed forward and down to the stone. She took the white man's head in her hands, and laid her own head on top of his.

"No!" she cried. She squeezed her eyes shut, and held her breath.

All the noise around her stopped at once. In the strange, sudden silence, Pocahontas lifted her head. She saw Tatacoope and the warriors stepping back in astonishment. She slowly looked back at her mother. Halewa had her hands pressed tightly over her mouth, and her eyes were full of fear.

Pocahontas looked up. Would she die now with the stranger? Her father raised his hand and gave a signal. Parahunt stepped close and bent over the stone, helping both Pocahontas and the white man to their feet. For just a moment she looked into the white man's face, and she was sure he recognized her. Parahunt led the prisoner toward the door.

Pocahontas looked again toward the throne, and her eyes met the glare of the old Quiyow. He tightened his lips, and squinted. Then he stalked out of the room after Parahunt.

Pocahontas's thoughts were in a jumble. What had she done? What would her father say?

He was staring at her, but not in fury. She could tell he was deep in thought. Finally he spoke up, in a solemn tone of voice she heard only at tribal councils.

"Matoaka," he said, "you have claimed the privilege of a princess." Only then did Pocahontas call to mind a rare custom among her people: Once in her life a maiden could claim deliverance for someone sentenced to die. The man whose life she claimed would become her elder brother. Remembering this made her mind spin even more.

Her father's forehead was wrinkled. His voice was quiet now and more familiar. "This mystery is a great one," he told her— "that you would use such a privilege on a stranger you've never seen." He shook his head.

Then he lifted his chin, and raised his hand over the people. He ended the gathering with a loud proclamation: "The prisoner John-Smith shall live!"

CHAPTER SIX

A FRIEND

LONG AFTER POCAHONTAS returned from the council long-house to her wigwam that night, she was still awake. She sat up straight on her sleeping mat, staring into the darkness. She was listening, listening for wisdom and understanding, as she had been taught.

The village had quickly become quiet. This would not be a long night of wild dancing, as it would have been if John-Smith had been killed to please Okewas.

Pocahontas had dared to raise her spirit against Okewas and against the Spirit Man. No doubt the Quiyow was simmering in anger tonight. His word had not been followed by Powhatan. Instead, the chief had shown greater regard for the request of a young girl. Pocahontas felt the fear again inside her. No doubt she had made an enemy tonight — an enemy who would want revenge.

She had been dangerously bold. But she wasn't sorry for what she did.

Pocahontas would probably do even more to displease the old Quiyow. After all, the blue-eyed man was her elder brother now. She was responsible for him. Since he was now a part of her people, he would need to learn their ways.

Finally, her heart calmed. She closed her eyes in sleep.

In the morning, after her bath with Little Otter in the cold river, she came back to the wigwam. From the bundle of her belongings she pulled out the white feather she had discovered yesterday. She found Parahunt, and asked him to take it as a gift to the white stranger. She hoped he would receive it as an offer of her help and friendship.

Soon Parahunt returned, and stood solemnly before her. "Princess Pocahontas," he announced, "this is the message I bring you: 'Ask the Princess to come to me, and I will give her blue beads.' That is what the man John-Smith says." Then Parahunt relaxed. He ruffled her hair, and smiled. "Come on, my little sister, and I'll take you to him."

As they walked together, Parahunt said, "Did you know you've given everyone in the village a wonderful new topic for gossip and argument? They all ask me: Why would the Princess want to save a Bearded One? And what is this meaning of this? Is it a sign of something good to come, or something evil? And I must give the same answer to all their questions: I don't know."

Pocahontas smiled and shook her head. She did not know, either. But she had prayed this morning that she could become stronger in spirit, to do whatever she must do.

At the edge of the village was a wigwam set apart for visitors to the tribe. Parahunt went to it, and stepped through the door. Pocahontas followed.

The white chief rose to his feet, and took both her hands in his. Pocahontas was glad to see him looking rested and well, so different from last night.

"Nay-hat-nah," he said slowly, in his rough Algonquin. "I am your friend." He raised his hands in the sign for friendship.

"Nay-hat-nah," she repeated. "I am your friend, Elder Brother."

She motioned for him to follow her outside. She would take him to see all of Comoco.

As they walked, he kept pointing at this or that, and she would tell him the Algonquin name for it. She also took him to meet her mother and Kahnessa and the Boy-with-no-name.

As they passed the council longhouse, the white chief came to a sudden stop. She saw him staring at the hundreds of scalps that hung on the fence around the meeting place. She was thankful for the darkness that kept him from seeing them last night, when his fate was uncertain. She hoped they did not make him fearful now. She took his arm, and gently pulled him in another direction.

The white man had many questions. "Parahunt told me that you're his sister," he said as they made their way to the river, "and that Chief Powhatan is your father. He also said Powhatan has many children."

She nodded. "Yes, eighty-seven."

"Where are they all?" he asked.

"They've been sent to other villages with their mothers. Sometimes my father grows tired of one of his wives, and he sends her away. But he always keeps his favorite children close by. He wants me here, and my mother Halewa has chosen to stay with me, though she no longer has favor in my father's eyes."

"And tell me this," the white man went on. "I know your people call us pale men and white strangers and the Bearded

Ones. But I've also heard them call us Tassen-tassees. What does that name mean?"

Pocahontas had to turn away. She was embarrassed.

"Please," the man John-Smith pleaded. "Don't be ashamed to tell me."

She looked back at him, then reluctantly bent down and traced a picture in the dirt with her finger. She drew a small animal with a stripe down its back. Then she pinched her nose to make sure he understood her drawing.

He nodded. "But why?" he asked.

She decided to tell him everything. "It's because of the smell of your people," she added. She was afraid he would be offended. But instead he laughed.

"It's true," he said. "I suppose we should take a bath more often."

At the river she introduced him to Little Otter. The Bearded One laughed again when he saw her pet launch himself out of the wintry water and come running into her arms. Nanoon and Kewelah were also there, and a few other children.

"This is where we come to bathe every morning, and to greet the sun and to pray," Pocahontas told the white man.

His face became serious. "This god you pray to — is it the one who wanted me dead last night?"

"No. Here we pray to Ahone, the Maker, the Creator God. We thank him for giving us all things. But it is Okewas who has power in this world. He is the War God who sends men into battle. He is served by the Quiyow, the Spirit Man who danced around you last night. Okewas can demand the sacrifice of human blood at any time."

"I, too, worship the Creator God," John-Smith said. "I

know there's also another spirit who loves war and the spilling of blood. But he's a devil spirit. He's the enemy of the Creator God."

Pocahontas tried not to show her surprise at such a strange notion. She wanted to know what the white chief meant, but she was afraid to ask about this.

Instead she asked about his magic arrow. He took it from around his neck and held it out to show her. It was true: The arrow floated inside the metal circle. It quivered, but no matter which way John-Smith turned it, it pointed back in the same direction — always northward.

"We call it a compass," he explained. "It saved my life when I was first captured, since everyone thought it was magic."

He hung the compass again around his neck, and added, "I almost forgot these." He reached into a pocket of his bulky clothing, and brought out the shiny blue beads he had promised. "For my new little sister," he said. He let them drop into her palms.

She smiled, and told him, "La-tee-nah."

CHAPTER SEVEN

DECISIONS

AS THE DAYS went by, Pocahontas saw John-Smith becoming more and more like her people. He often went hunting with the braves. Parahunt said he was learning fast to use the bow.

Mother Halewa kept the white chief well fed. Pocahontas smiled to see how he devoured corncakes and maple sugar, and how he chose the biggest clamshell spoon to eat Halewa's deer's-head soup. Once she heard John-Smith tell her mother that he was eating far better than anyone did in the white men's village.

"The white chief is worried about his people," Halewa said to Pocahontas that night as they lay down in their wigwam. "They are hungry."

The next day, after he and Parahunt returned from a morning hunt, she sat down with John-Smith on a low stone beside her mother's cooking fire. He was holding the white feather Pocahontas had given him. He had a smooth piece of wood, and had borrowed a small clay pot filled with the dye Halewa made from berry juice. He dipped the end of the feather in the berry-dye, and made strange marks with it on the piece of wood.

"This," he said, "is your name."

She wondered if he meant the white feather. How did he know her secret name? But no, he was pointing to the marks he had made.

"These are letters," he said, "and together they say the name Pocahontas. With letters and words like this, I can send a message to anyone anywhere, and I can say as much as I want to."

She didn't see how this could be. "My father sends his messages by runners," she told him. "Even if Powhatan speaks all morning long, the runner will remember every word, and he'll deliver my father's message perfectly."

"That's truly a wonder," John-Smith agreed. "But the words made with these marks can last longer than any messenger. Right now I could mark down a message that tells everything about Powhatan. It could be saved and given to his great-grandchildren and even their great-grandchildren. A hundred years from now it would still be there in these marks, for everyone to understand — the same message.

"I could even send a message about you to my people in England far across the ocean. I can tell them how Princess Pocahontas looks, and what she wears, and what she does each day, and how she saved my life — all that with marks just like these."

Pocahontas shook her head. This was a mystery. Yes, the new Elder Brother was becoming a good Algonquin, but she saw there were also many things to learn from the white men.

"Tell me about this England across the great water," she asked him.

"The houses are made of stones," he told her. "And girls like you wear dresses that stick out wide, like little wigwams."

She wondered if he was teasing her. Why would anyone dress like that?

"I've sailed on the oceans to see many other lands, too," John-Smith continued. "But of all the places I've seen, this is the finest of all. When I stepped from our ship I found strawberries four times bigger than those we have in England. The trees are so tall here, and the woods are filled with animals. The rivers are mighty and filled with fish. I love your land, Pocahontas."

"It's your land, now," she answered. "You'll stay here, with us, as my adopted brother. You're family now."

She saw lines of worry cross his forehead. "But my people in our village — in Jamestown — I know they need me. Some of our chiefs aren't as wise as they should be. They care more about hunting for gold than hunting for food."

Pocahontas wanted to close her mind to these words. She wished he would forget the village he called Jamestown. Besides, didn't the Brothers say this village could not last long against sickness and ocean storms? But John-Smith would become a mighty Algonquin.

At sunset three nights later, the drums sounded again for a tribal gathering. Painted warriors went to the guest wigwam to summon the white man. Pocahontas walked beside him to the council longhouse. He hadn't been in that room since the night he was nearly killed. She hoped he wasn't afraid now. She was sure tonight's council was not about war. After all, not once had she seen the Quiyow since the night John-Smith's life was spared.

The warriors inside the longhouse stood at attention before Powhatan's throne. From head to toe they were all painted black, the color that meant solemn tribal matters were being decided.

Chief Powhatan offered a peace pipe of burning tobacco to John-Smith. Pocahontas saw him inhale the smoke slowly and ceremoniously. He had learned well.

Her father towered silently above him. His chin was lifted. His eyes were narrowed. He always looked this way in times of great decision.

At last Powhatan spoke.

"John-Smith, I know you are one of the chiefs of your people, the Bearded Ones."

John-Smith nodded.

"You stand before me today because of the desire of my favored daughter to redeem you. Because of what she did, you have traded the sentence of death for the spirit of adoption. You are now Algonquin. You are one of us. You are the Elder Brother of Pocahontas. I name you Nantaquod — the Adopted One.

"Though a child, Pocahontas has taken on a great responsibility. But she has long been on the path to becoming a Spirit Woman."

At these words, Pocahontas squared her shoulders and stood taller.

"Now I've made a decision," Powhatan announced. "I've decided that trade with the Bearded Ones is better than war.

"You became a chief among the Bearded Ones; therefore you are now a chief among the Algonquin. As an adopted chief you must favor me, as my other chiefs favor me. You must show your allegiance to me with gifts.

"I will tell you the gifts that please me. And you will return to your home village."

Beside her, Pocahontas heard John-Smith take a quick breath at the same time she did.

"Tonight," Chief Powhatan declared, "I will send you back to your village. Twelve of my honored warriors will go with you.

When you send the warriors back to me, I ask you to also send gifts.

"I ask for one of your grinding stones, for you have told my daughter and her mother of the fine ones you have in your village. I ask for pots of copper. And I ask for the gift of two giant thunder-sticks that shoot fire. With these, I will be strong against my enemies the Iroquois and the mighty Huron. These are the gifts a chief such as you must send a king such as me."

"Great Powhatan," John-Smith replied, "I am honored by my adoption. I am honored to be counted as an Algonquin chief. I am honored to be able to return to my village so I may send you the gifts you desire."

Pocahontas felt her heart sinking. She did not want Elder Brother to leave.

"Yet I have one request," he went on. "Chief Powhatan, it would please me greatly if you would allow the Princess Pocahontas to travel with me tonight, back to my village."

Her eyes flew to meet those of her father.

John-Smith Nantaquod continued. "I would like very much to give the Princess special gifts. I would like her to be a guest in our village for a few days. We will treat her as a princess among our people. And she may return at your bidding."

Chief Powhatan was standing with his arms folded. He nodded his head in consent.

She could go! With her own eyes she would see this strange tribe and all their ways.

John-Smith stepped out at once to return to his wigwam and gather his belongings for the night journey. Pocahontas stepped up to her father's throne. With thankfulness singing in her heart, she bent forward and touched her forehead to her father's folded arms.

CHAPTER EIGHT

A MIRACLE

ON THE MOONLIT WATERS, the long canoe glided silently. Parahunt was in front, and Remcoe was at the rear. In the middle sat Pocahontas. She wore a rabbit-skin cloak to keep out the evening coolness.

Parahunt stopped paddling. Over his shoulder, he looked back at Pocahontas. Then he lifted his paddle and held it out to her. "You've always wanted to go on a journey of adventure, Little Sister. Would you enjoy it more if you got to paddle?"

She nodded eagerly.

"Just think," he said, as she parted the waters with her first smooth stroke. "This time you don't even have to hide under an old bearskin."

Her laugh echoed on the shimmering waters.

They were going down the river to the Chesapeake. From there they would go upstream on the next river south, the river that Jamestown was on. With them in the canoe were baskets of cornmeal and dried berries and nuts, plus the meat of deer and bear, and a string of dried fish. The food was a gift to the white men in John-Smith's village.

Pocahontas was thinking of Elder Brother and the twelve warriors with him. At this same moment they were taking the shorter but more tiring way from Comoco to Jamestown. They were on foot, traveling southward through the forest. They went over land so they could come back that way with the heavy thunder-sticks that shot fire.

She thought of how glad the men at Jamestown would be to see John-Smith return, since he had been away for more than two moons.

The morning sun was reflected on the water when the canoe finally beached on the riverbank at the white men's village. John-Smith and the twelve warriors had walked swiftly and had already arrived. With them on the riverbank were several of the Bearded Ones.

Stepping on shore, Pocahontas recognized English words that John-Smith had taught her. "Food!" the white men were saying. "They have food!"

"Yes," Pocahontas told them. "Food." She held her open hand toward the supplies in the canoe, indicating for the Bearded Ones to accept the gift. Several of them began unloading the food and carrying it inside the log wall that surrounded their village.

John-Smith Nantaquod welcomed Pocahontas to Jamestown, and said, "Your father's braves have asked to see how the giant thunder-sticks work before they carry them back to your father. I'll show them now." He led the way to the thunder-sticks. The Bearded Ones called them "cannon."

Several thunder-sticks guarded the gate into the village. Pocahontas saw the white men put gray powder inside one of them.

John-Smith motioned for everyone to stand back.

BOOM! the thunder-stick shouted, and the earth around them shook. Most of Powhatan's braves fell backward to the ground in fear. Parahunt and Pocahontas had stayed standing, but only by holding on to John-Smith's shoulders.

"It's good! It's powerful and good!" the warriors shouted, as they regained their courage and gathered around the English weapon. "King Powhatan will be pleased."

"Then you may return to King Powhatan now with two of our thunder-sticks," John-Smith told them.

Six of the warriors surrounded one thunder-stick, and six others surrounded a second one. They wrapped their arms around them and began to pull. Nothing happened. Then all twelve joined together to try to move one thunder-stick. The muscles in their arms and backs were tight and bulging.

"Pull!" John-Smith shouted. "Pull harder!"

As her father's men continued to struggle, Pocahontas watched her friend John-Smith with growing understanding. He must have foreseen this all along, she realized. It would take many more men than twelve to move the thunder-sticks any-where. All the Bearded Ones must have worked together to pull them here up the riverbank from the ships that brought them from England.

"I'm sorry. I'm so sorry," John-Smith told the warriors when they finally gave up in disgust. "I'll put the grinding stone and the copper pots in Parahunt's canoe. At least those can be taken."

These gifts as well as some beautiful beads were brought out from the village and loaded in the canoe. John-Smith also gave a hunting knife to Remcoe, and a shining axe to Parahunt.

Grumbling with disappointment, the twelve other warriors began the walk back to Comoco. Meanwhile, beside the canoe at the riverbank, John-Smith Nantaquod grasped the hands of Parahunt and Remcoe, and touched their shoulders in friendship.

"I'll take good care of Princess Pocahontas," he promised her brother. "I'll give her gifts that please her. You may come for her whenever Powhatan decides."

Pocahontas called goodbye to Parahunt and Remcoe as their canoe slid away.

Then she turned with John-Smith and walked up the riverbank and through the gate of his village. Her eyes were open wide to every detail. Bearded Ones were all around. They looked tired and weak, and many looked sick. Their smell helped her understand at once why her people called them Tassen-tassees.

She heard John-Smith introducing her as Princess Matoaka Pocahontas, daughter of the mighty Powhatan. The white men bent forward in stiff bows, and spoke English words that she didn't know.

"They're saying how grateful they are for the food," John-Smith said. "They'll prepare a fine dinner for everyone tonight."

She smiled, and tried an awkward bow in return.

The wooden shelters in the village seemed miraculous to Pocahontas, with their sides so straight and tall. The roofs were made of matted sticks and grass. John-Smith called it "thatch." Around the village were many tools and other things she did not understand.

She had seen no women anywhere. "Where are your maidens?" she asked John-Smith.

"We brought no women with us," he answered.

"No women! That's why you're all hungry! Only women know how to raise corn and beans. My sisters and I could have shown you how."

"The men have been unable to plant anything outside the walls," he explained. "They were afraid of arrows from the Paspeg warriors."

He introduced her to a gray-haired man he called Reverend Hunt. He was the Spirit Man in Jamestown, but he wore no snakes or weasel skins. Pocahontas was amazed at how cheerful he seemed, even though he appeared weaker and sicker than the others.

She also met a man named Percy, a slender man who smiled and kissed her hand. Percy and Reverend Hunt were giving friendly slaps to John-Smith's back, and smiled with him. But Pocahontas noticed that most of the other men didn't seem happy about his return. When they talked with John-Smith, their tone was grave. Then they stared at him and whispered to one another.

Two of the troubled men seemed to be chiefs. John-Smith told her their names. A puffy looking man was named Ratcliffe, and the other, who reminded her of a puny dog, was named Archer. John-Smith said these two had been chosen as leaders among the Bearded Ones.

She was led inside a house that John-Smith said was for eating. A table made of smooth, polished wood was in the center. On one side of the house a special place had been built from stone to hold the fire, so the smoke didn't hang heavy inside. A black pot with something cooking inside was on the fire. Several men came in to eat.

The awful smell of these men — all together in a closed room — almost made her cover her nose.

Even here at the table together, the men seemed uncomfortable with John-Smith. She sat next to him. She was offered a metal spoon, shiny and smooth, and a bowl of watery soup. John-Smith called it gruel. She could get down only one swallow. If this was all the Bearded Ones had to eat, it was no wonder they were weak and hungry. She was glad for the food that came in the canoe. It would make a royal feast tonight.

After the meager meal, she gladly followed Elder Brother out of the stuffy, smelly room. She climbed with him to the top of a tower built in a corner of the wall. They could look out at everything in and around Jamestown. He let Pocahontas look through a magical round stick that he called a "spy-glass." It made faraway things look close.

While they were alone on the lookout tower, John-Smith explained his situation. "The other chiefs are angry with me. One of them — Archer — is saying that I must be punished."

"Punished? For what?" she asked.

"For the death of the men who followed me into the forest when I was captured."

"But it was the Pamunkeys and my Uncle Opech who killed those men. There is nothing you could have done to save them!"

"Yes, I know. But Archer and Ratcliffe are jealous of me. They don't like me, because some of the men would rather follow my orders than theirs. They thought I was dead and gone. Now they want to get rid of me for sure."

From down below came a shout: "Captain Smith!"

Elder Brother exchanged words with the soldier who had shouted. Then he turned to Pocahontas. "They want to talk to me, in Ratcliffe's house," he said. She followed him down the ladder.

He was taken inside one of the shelters. The wooden door slammed shut.

Pocahontas waited outside. She swayed and quietly groaned. The Spirit Man, Reverend Hunt, came to stand with her. He spoke no Algonquin words, but she was glad to have him nearby.

Finally, the wooden door opened, and several men came out. Elder Brother was between Ratcliffe and Archer. His blue eyes were dark, and his hands were bound behind his back.

Pocahontas rushed toward him. He spoke to her in Algonquin. "They've decided I must die," he said.

"Die?" She repeated the word with unbelief.

"Don't fear, Little Sister," Nantaquod said. "They've promised to return you to your father unharmed. They understand how important you are."

Pocahontas immediately started wailing. Some of the Bearded Ones scowled at her. "Hush!" they shouted.

But she wailed louder. How could this be happening? In her own village she had been able to save John-Smith. But in this place she was powerless, and Parahunt and the others were long gone.

Reverend Hunt laid his arm around John-Smith's shoulder, and the two men knelt together in the dirt. They closed their eyes and bowed their heads, and spoke quietly.

Pocahontas saw a Bearded One hanging a rope from a beam extending from the lookout tower. At the end of it dangled a loop.

She let her voice call out loudly in prayer. "Ahone, Creator God, hear us! O God of Nantaquod, save him!"

Other Bearded Ones crowded around. They seemed quiet and numb. Even Percy, John-Smith's friend, looked weak and confused. Pocahontas saw that no one there could help Elder Brother.

Then there came a shout from the Bearded One on the look-out tower. His face was turned toward the river.

Suddenly there was a sound like thunder — like a boom made by one of the thunder-sticks, but farther away.

A cry rang out: "A ship! A ship!"

Everyone was cheering and running out through the gate, leaving John-Smith behind. Percy and Reverend Hunt at once began untying the rope around his hands. Pocahontas ran forward and threw her arms around her friend. His face was bathed in relief. "It's an English ship that was due here months ago," he explained. "I think everything will be all right now."

She heard him repeating an English word she didn't know: "A miracle!" he exclaimed. "A miracle for me, and for us all!"

CHAPTER NINE

TO THE STOREHOUSE

SOON POCAHONTAS and Elder Brother joined the cheering crowd of Bearded Ones at the river's edge. She was awed by the sight of the huge ship. The sails were like giant swans swimming together up the wide river.

The ship stopped far out in the water. Soon a much smaller boat came from it, with six Bearded Ones inside. As soon as the boat reached the shore, one of the men who stepped from it seemed to command everyone's respect and attention — even puffy Ratcliffe and the puny dog Archer. John-Smith told her the man was called Captain Newport.

"And this is the royal Princess Pocahontas," Elder Brother said to him.

Captain Newport bowed to her and said, "How beautiful you are, my child."

All the Bearded Ones seemed to be talking at the same time to Captain Newport. John-Smith and Ratcliffe and Archer and others walked with him through the gate.

One of the men was returning in the smaller boat to the ship. Pocahontas sat down on the grassy bank and stared out across the water. *So this is what carries Bearded Ones across the Great Gray Ocean,* she thought. And now, she reasoned, the Swan Boat would take the soldiers of Jamestown back to England, where they could be with their women, and be happier and in good health. Elder Brother, meanwhile, would stay here in the land he liked better than England or any other place. Here he would become a mighty Algonquin.

Across the water, she saw men rolling up the sails on high poles that towered above the ship. Now it no longer made her think of giant swans, but of a boat with trees growing out of it.

Soon the small boat was coming back again to shore. It was crowded with more men. She stayed long on the riverbank and watched the boat going back and forth from ship to shore. She counted seventy new Tassen-tassees who had come to Jamestown, including two boys who looked her own age. All the new arrivals appeared stronger and healthier than the men already in Jamestown. She quickly decided the English must have come to stay. She wondered what her father would think about that.

That night everyone feasted on the food Pocahontas had provided, plus a biting drink called rum that was brought from the ship. After the meal came singing and dancing. There were no drums, but one man held a wooden box with strings stretched along it, and pulled a long stick across the strings to make a singing sound. The box was a fiddle, John-Smith said. The fast, happy noises made the soldiers tap their boots and clap their hands.

Another soldier brought out an even stranger noise-maker. It seemed to be a bag of wind, and sounded like a hundred wolves howling. Pocahontas wanted to cover her ears. When John-

Smith saw how much it troubled her, he asked the man playing it to move to the other side of the room.

The next morning she again saw the little boat going back and forth from the ship. This time it brought supplies of food instead of more people. Back inside the village wall, she watched as most of the food was carried into what the English called a storehouse. The work went on throughout the day.

With everyone so busy around her, and not much to do herself, Pocahontas began turning cartwheels just outside the storehouse. Out from the storehouse door came the two boys her age. They laughed and started cartwheeling too, until one of the soldiers shouted for them. They had to hurry to the riverbank to help carry more supplies.

Alone now, Pocahontas tossed herself into another string of cartwheels, six of them this time. When she stopped, she was in front of an open door in the building next to the storehouse. Through the door, in the back of the shelter, she saw the village's Spirit Man, Reverend Hunt. He saw her as well, and motioned for her to come inside.

At first she dared not enter. Among her people, the Spirit Men always kept apart. It was unheard of for the Quiyow to invite anyone into his wigwam, and certainly not a child.

Pocahontas couldn't imagine any child wanting to go inside a Quiyow's dwelling. But something inside her wanted to accept this invitation from the white Spirit Man. She had already seen Reverend Hunt walking among his people, smiling and speaking just as if he were one of them. She had seen him praying with John-Smith, and comforting him. Surely he was no danger to her.

She stepped inside. She made her way past slabs of wood laid across wood-stubs and arranged in rows. Reverend Hunt was sitting in a chair near the back. Above him on the wall were two pieces of silver put together. One piece was upright, and the other crossed it at the center. Now she remembered: Yesterday when she and John-Smith had walked by, he pointed out this meeting place where the white men worshiped God. He called it their "church."

At the center of the room, the roof sloped high to the inside of a tower. She looked up. At the top, hanging upside down, was something that looked like a pot made of metal. Inside it was a metal stick, with a rope tied to it. The rope hung down not far above her head.

Reverend Hunt rose from his chair and came beside her. He reached for the rope-end, and gave it a pull. High in the tower she saw the metal pot jerk, as if it were trying to get rightside-up again. The metal stick crashed into the side of it. The sound it made filled her heart with wonder.

"Bell," Reverend Hunt said.

He walked back to his chair. He picked up something she had seen him holding in his lap when she first came in. "Bible," he said. She could tell this Bible was of great value to him, from the way he carefully held it out to her. The top was white with lines on it. Looking closer, she saw that the lines were rows and rows of black markings like the ones John-Smith showed her.

She held the Bible in her open palms. The bottom was like soft deerskin. Reverend Hunt used his thumb to show her that the top was made of stacks of thin white sheets, far thinner than birchbark could ever be. There were two stacks of the thin sheets, side by side, but brought together somehow in the middle. On every sheet she saw, there were more tiny rows of black markings. She guessed that this must be a message of many, many words. But she wondered who had marked it, and how he could have made the marks so small.

Reverend Hunt was saying something, but she didn't understand. Then she caught a few English words she knew: "God," "good," "Creator." John-Smith had taught her these words when they talked about Ahone. Perhaps the words in this Bible were from the Creator God. Was it possible that he himself had marked this message?

Not long before sundown Elder Brother told her that there would be another feast that evening. The new supplies for Jamestown had been moved off the ship and into the storehouse. To celebrate, Captain Newport had invited the leaders of Jamestown to be his guests for dinner on the ship. "And Princess Pocahontas is invited as well," John-Smith told her.

The first star of the night began shining while she and John-Smith were out in the smaller boat in the river. Against the sky's last bit of blue, she could see the outline of the bare, towering tree-poles that grew up out of the Swan Boat. She could hardly hold in her excitement about getting to visit the giant ship, as she came closer to it. But when she was finally helped up from the smaller boat onto the bigger one, her excitement began dying away. The Tassen-tassee smell was even worse here than in the village. It grew stronger as they stepped inside the belly of the ship, down into a room where their dinner was spread before them on a table.

Pocahontas and John-Smith sat between his friend Percy and Captain Newport. Elder Brother told her that Percy's brother had made himself an enemy to King James, the great chief of England. Percy had been afraid for his own life. That's why he had come across the ocean to this land.

Captain Newport seemed delighted with her. John-Smith told Pocahontas that she reminded Captain Newport of his own daughters across the sea.

Pocahontas noticed that Archer and Ratcliffe were not at the meal. Elder Brother told her that Captain Newport was angry with them, and would try to punish them. "He's a wise man and a strong leader," John-Smith said. Pocahontas realized she had learned a lesson about the Bearded Ones. There were both wise chiefs and foolish chiefs here, just as there were among her own people.

Just then a cry rang out from the top of the ship: "Fire in the village!"

Pocahontas followed as everyone hurried up to look across the water. They saw tongues of flames leaping up from one of the thatch roofs inside the village wall.

The smaller boat quickly filled up with men who hurried to go back. Halfway across the water she heard someone calling back to the ship: "It's the storehouse! The storehouse is on fire!"

It was later that night before Pocahontas got back across the river to the village. She stood with the gloomy men of Jamestown around a huge pile of glowing cinders and ashes. This was all that was left of the storehouse and of the food carried all the way from England.

The Brothers had been right all along, Pocahontas decided. The white men's village could not survive.

The church next to the storehouse had burned as well. She saw Reverend Hunt squatting beside its ruins. He covered his face with his hands.

At that moment in the smoky darkness, Pocahontas realized how much she did not want Jamestown to disappear. She wanted the Bearded Ones to stay and to live, and to be well and happy. But she knew that only her own people could keep them from dying.

CHAPTER TEN

GENTLE JAILER

THE LONG FOREST PATH between Comoco and Jamestown soon became the one Pocahontas knew best. She often took as many as twelve other children with her to carry gifts of food to the hungry Bearded Ones. She was happy to do this.

She was even happier that her father had asked his people to trade with the Bearded Ones. Because of this, much of her people's corn had made its way to Jamestown.

On one warm evening, Chief Powhatan summoned her to a meal of crabcakes in the council longhouse. She was his only guest. They sat cross-legged on either side of the food. Draping from her father's shoulders was a new buckskin mantle she had sewn for him, with Halewa's help.

Pocahontas could tell this was a solemn time. She said nothing. She must wait until her father spoke first.

Pocahontas remembered the excitement in this room on a night not long ago. Elder Brother was here with Captain Newport and many soldiers from Jamestown. The Bearded Ones gave gifts to her father and his family: blue beads and copper bracelets and rolls of something red called velvet, which was softer than the softest deerskin. They also gave him a wondrous dog, a greyhound. It was the fastest animal she had ever seen, and her father named him Kint.

Pocahontas had been especially surprised to see the two white boys she had known in Jamestown. One of them, named Thomas, was to stay here at Comoco to serve Powhatan and his people, and to learn their ways. The other boy, Samuel, would stay for a while at another of Powhatan's villages. In return, Chief Powhatan allowed his son Namontack to be a helper for Captain Newport. Later that night, John-Smith told Pocahontas that Namontack might even sail with Captain Newport across the ocean.

Now Pocahontas began wondering what Namontack would see if he went to England. She imagined what she might see and do, if only she could go there too.

The voice of Powhatan startled her from her daydream. The crabcakes were eaten, and he was speaking his first words: "Can you save your own people, Pocahontas? Can you save them like you saved Nantaquod?"

"What do you mean, Father?"

"The Tassen-tassees have captured ten of our best warriors," he answered. "They are prisoners in the white village. Your brother Tatacoope is one of them."

She could hardly believe what she heard.

"But why?" she asked. "How could the Bearded Ones do it?"

Her father's face grew stern. "They are angry at us," he said, "because we demanded what is right. I am weary of trading corn for copper and beads. I want swords and guns. When the Bearded Ones brought their gifts here, I told them we would now trade only for swords and guns. And that is what our warriors tried to take from them."

So weapons were the root of this problem, Pocahontas realized. She was not sure that even her friendship with Elder Brother could help now. But she would try.

"I will fast and pray to Ahone for a day," she said. "Then I will go."

She stood. As she stepped toward the door, her father called out, "In two days we will offer the spring sacrifice to Okewas. Is it right for you to be away?"

Pocahontas shuddered inwardly. Once again Okewas was demanding blood. A picture flashed into her mind. She saw the black-painted old Quiyow stretching out his hand. His voice wailed. His finger pointed. It pointed to Lominas, her cousin, her friend. Halewa had quickly pulled Pocahontas behind her to hide her eyes at the moment of sacrifice. But Mother had not covered her daughter's ears. Pocahontas could never forget the screams of Lominas, Lominas-who-was-no-more.

Now she felt hot tears in her eyes as she looked back to her father. He seemed lost in thought, and wasn't looking at her. "But perhaps," he finally said, "it cannot be helped. Go, Pocahontas, and do what you can."

She nodded, and silently gave thanks to the Creator God for her father's change of mind about her missing the sacrifice.

In her secret place by the river the next day, she hugged her knees to her chest and rested her chin on her arms. She was watching Little Otter play.

He had grown hot in the sunshine. He slid back into the water and swam in a rapid circle, leaving a silvery wake. Then he popped back out of the water and cooled her with a shaking spray. Once again he jumped into the river and sped away. She could see him through the rippling current, playfully rolling over and over along the river bottom.

She laughed. "You're tempting me to play, I know," she called, when he showed his head above the surface. "But you're also reminding me of something, aren't you?"

Little Otter was the king of his Water World. He was the fastest swimmer and the best fisherman in the river. But he also loved the World of Land. He sunned himself in the spring and summer. In the winter he would slide and play in the snow.

"You're at home in two worlds," she said. "And I am like you. Pocahontas also lives in two worlds."

A day later, she entered the familiar clearing that had been cut from the forest around Jamestown. The guard on the lookout tower waved a greeting. "It's Pocahontas!" he shouted cheerfully to the others inside the wall.

As usual, Elder Brother met her at the gate. As they walked inside the village, Pocahontas glanced at the building the Bearded Ones called the stockade. She knew her tribesmen must be inside it. Two guards stood outside the door, holding guns.

That night she was seated at a small table in John-Smith's house. Reverend Hunt and Percy were also there.

Pocahontas bowed her head while the Spirit Man said a prayer of thanksgiving to the Creator God. Pocahontas was praying too, and praying hard. If she failed in her mission to free the Algonquins, she believed an attack on Jamestown was certain. Many lives would be lost.

Pocahontas held her metal spoon and ate from it exactly as she had learned from the Bearded Ones. Tonight's meal was a soup made with clams.

From the three men she learned of all that had happened

since her last visit. Captain Newport had sailed back across the ocean. Her half-brother Namontack went with him. Captain Newport had also taken Archer with him, to leave him in England before Captain Newport returned to Jamestown as soon as he could. Ratcliffe was still in the village, but the men looked to John-Smith now as their leader.

This was good news. If her own Elder Brother was the true chief of Jamestown, her mission had a greater chance to succeed.

"As you know," John-Smith remarked, "Ratcliffe has always been very strict. Last winter he put a man to death for stealing food from the storehouse. But of course, stealing must always be punished severely." He was looking at Pocahontas when he said this.

The men kept talking. Finally, when they were quiet, she spoke.

"My friend and Elder Brother, you must know that my father has sent me."

"Yes," he answered. "I'm sure Chief Powhatan sent you to ask about the prisoners."

"They are my kinsmen," she said, "and among them is my brother."

"They were stealing," he replied. "What would your father say if we came into Comoco and tried to take away his warclubs and his bows and arrows?"

She answered truthfully. "He would say you deserved to die." She paused, and chose her words carefully. "But I have come to ask you for mercy, Elder Brother."

It was long before John-Smith answered. "I was a prisoner once," he said. His forehead was tight with seriousness. "And I had a gentle jailer. She watched over me carefully. She taught me the ways of her people. Now, if I could only find that same jailer again, I would let her take charge of these prisoners we have. That way, none of our soldiers would need to bother about guarding the stockade."

Pocahontas was confused by his words. Then she saw that his blue eyes were sparkling.

"Pocahontas, I owe you my life," he went on. "I cannot deny your request for the prisoners' freedom. But as you take these men to your father, you must be a gentle but wise jailer, and make sure they do not make this mistake again. We cannot allow stealing.

"Tell your father," he continued, "that John Smith Nantaquod is a man of his word. Tell him that I have greatly honored my adoption as your Elder Brother by releasing his warriors unharmed."

The next day was a day of rest for the white men, and John Smith said he would not release the prisoners that day. The wonderful bell in the new church rang, and the Bearded Ones gathered there. Pocahontas waited just outside the door. She liked the singing that floated out of the building with such strange melody.

The next morning Pocahontas led the ten warriors away from Jamestown. All of them were well and unharmed. Tatacoope alone looked angry. She knew he hated being rescued by his little sister.

When they neared Comoco, the villagers ran out to meet them. Pocahontas was lifted on the shoulders of the tallest braves, and the people cheered.

Even Powhatan came out to greet her. "You have done well, Pocahontas," he said.

Back inside the village, she went first to her wigwam. Her

mother was inside, and her little brother was napping on his sleeping mat.

"Look, Mother," Pocahontas whispered. "I've brought you a special gift from John-Smith." She held out a mirror.

Halewa smiled for a moment as she took the mirror. But soon her face was sad again.

Pocahontas spoke the hated question that she could not help asking. "Who was chosen this time in the Dark Magic?"

"Little Melon-Belly, the child of Dawinta," her mother answered.

Pocahontas gasped in horror. "But he was so young!"

Halewa gently stroked the back of her own sleeping child. "Yes," she said, "only a baby."

CHAPTER ELEVEN

FEVER SEASON

PARAHUNT AND POCAHONTAS were walking along the forest trail from Comoco toward Jamestown. It was the time of year called Thunder Moon, though Pocahontas had heard the Bearded Ones calling it July.

Back at Comoco, the corn had grown high. Today it was her sister Kahnessa's turn to keep the birds and other creatures away from all the crops. When Parahunt told Pocahontas he wanted to go to Jamestown and show Nantaquod how to spear the river sturgeon, she was free to go along. She was eager to be with her brother, because he was soon leaving Comoco to become the chief at another Algonquin village beyond Jamestown.

She was glad that Parahunt, unlike Tatacoope, seemed to share her desire to keep learning more from the white men, even as the Tassen-tassees were eager to learn from the Algonquins. "Some of the Bearded Ones are good," Parahunt had said. "I like Nantaquod."

As they neared Jamestown, she was thrilled to see the lushness of the fields around the village walls. She and Kahnessa had helped the Bearded Ones plant several rows of corn and beans, and they made mounds for squash and melons. To Pocahontas, the fast-growing crops were like a picture of her own growth in learning white men's ways. She understood their English words well now, and could talk with any of the men.

She and Parahunt also passed by the white men's graveyard in a meadow beside the growing corn. It had more wooden crosses than Pocahontas could quickly count. Some of them were on mounds of fresh earth. Thunder Moon was often a season of sickness and fever and dying, especially here in the lowland.

Parahunt quickly found John-Smith and told him about the mighty sturgeon. As Elder Brother went off with Parahunt, he said to Pocahontas, "You may want to visit Reverend Hunt. I'm afraid he isn't well."

She made her way to the new church, and walked in. At one end of the room was a small glass window Captain Newport had given to the people of Jamestown. The sunlight made it shine red and blue. The dazzling colored light made this her favorite place in Jamestown.

Reverend Hunt lay on his narrow bed in a side-room within the church. He lifted his head as she entered, and smiled weakly. "Welcome, child," he said.

She took his hand. It was trembling and hot.

He struggled to talk. "It seems there's been no trouble between your people and mine," he said, "since you took back the captured warriors."

"Yes," she answered. "There is peace."

"You did well, my child. You're a peacemaker. And blessed are the peacemakers."

"Blessed?" she said. "What is this word?"

He smiled. "It means happy. Happy are the peacemakers. Jesus taught us this."

"I often hear you speak of this Jesus," she said. "Who is he?"

"He is the Son of Ahone. The Creator God sent his own Son into this world to overcome the power of the evil one."

"Did he fight with Okewas?" she asked.

"In his own way, yes. Jesus let the evil one come against him and kill him. Jesus was the perfect blood-sacrifice. He was buying our life by giving up his own. The word we use is *redeem*. He was redeeming us.

"It's like what you were willing to do, Pocahontas. Captain Smith told us how you laid down your head on top of his, to save him from the sacrifice to Okewas. Jesus did that for us. He came between us and the evil one, so the evil one could not have us."

Reverend Hunt closed his eyes, and breathed hard. She saw how much strength he had spent in explaining this to her. She held his hand more tightly in both of hers, trying to give him her own strength so he could keep talking.

He looked at her, and nodded. "I — I will speak more to you, my child. There's so much to tell you. The story of Jesus doesn't end with his death…" Reverend Hunt could not go on. He closed his eyes again, and turned his head.

She was afraid for him.

She stepped away from his bed, and walked out of the church into the burning summer sun of the fever season.

Three mornings later when the sun rose again, she stood beside Parahunt and Elder Brother as Reverend Hunt's body was lowered into a new grave in the meadow beside the corn. She did not wail, as her own people did when someone was buried. She stood still and silent, though tears rolled down her cheeks. She wondered who would tell her the rest of the story that Reverend Hunt knew about Jesus.

Throughout the summer Pocahontas kept up her visits to Jamestown. Until the crops were harvested, she and her sisters brought gifts of corn every few days. They also brought herbs and medicines, and tended to the Tassen-tassees who were sick with fever.

Now and then she heard the men calling her a new name. The word was strange.

"What is this they're calling me?" she asked John-Smith one day.

"They have named you Nonpareil," he answered. "It's a French word, from another of our languages. And it means that there's no one like you. There is no one equal to your charm and your courage. There is no one like the Princess Pocahontas!"

CHAPTER TWELVE

UNWANTED CROWN

IT WAS NOT YET DAYLIGHT, but someone was shaking Pocahontas awake. She struggled to open her eyes. She saw Kahnessa,
pulling at her and whispering, "Wake up, Matoaka!"

"What is it?"

"Little Otter is in danger," Kahnessa answered. "Come
quick."

Pocahontas slipped silently out of the wigwam and hurried
with her sister down the well-worn river path. The first full
moon of the fall was shining through the trees. It made patches
of light on the forest floor.

"I couldn't sleep," Kahnessa told her. "So I walked to the
river. And there I saw what Little Otter had done."

The moon was bright on the river. Kahnessa pointed toward
the fish traps. Only yesterday Tatacoope had placed several new
basket-traps here, and Pocahontas knew how much he was looking forward to his first catch in the morning.

She stepped closer to see. The new traps had been raided. The baskets had been shredded and torn, and were empty of fish.

"But how do you know Little Otter did this?" Pocahontas cried out. "He catches his own food!"

"I saw him," Kahnessa answered. "I drove him away myself. Oh, my sister! Now Tatacoope will catch Little Otter and skin him for sure."

Pocahontas sat on the bank and forced herself to think. A few fireflies circled around her head, giving off their soft greenish glow. "No," she finally decided. "I'll take him away — far away. You must tell Tatacoope that you drove him up the river with rocks. And tell Mother that in sorrow for Little Otter, I have gone to see my friends in Jamestown."

"But where will you take him?"

"I'll go beyond Jamestown, to the village where Parahunt is now chief. I'll leave Little Otter in the river there."

Pocahontas stood and said, "I must go at once."

She walked along the bank, whistling for her pet. In a moment she heard him bark. As he leaped out of the water and threw himself playfully at her feet, she scolded him with anger mixed with sorrow. She gathered him in her arms.

"I must send you away, Little Otter," she whispered. "You must start a new life. Perhaps you'll even find a mate."

She carried her pet to the canoe which Parahunt had left behind to be her own. She could handle a canoe now as skillfully as the Brothers. Little Otter scampered into the bow and she pushed off.

The sun was high when Pocahontas came to Parahunt's village. He greeted her warmly and introduced her to his new wife.

Then he walked beside his sister down to the stream with Little Otter.

She let him jump from her arms into the waters of his new home. Parahunt laughed as Little Otter swam in quick circles, then took a dive and rolled over and over beneath the surface.

"He'll be happy here," Parahunt said, "as I am."

"Your wife is lovely," Pocahontas responded. "But she looks so young."

"Only two summers older than you," he answered. "Soon, my little sister, Father will see that you're engaged to a great warrior from another of his tribes."

"But I'm his favorite daughter. Father said I'll be a Spirit Woman, and I can rule my own village."

Parahunt smiled. "Yes, all that will happen. But he also wants you to help keep his kingdom strong. You can do that best if you marry the warrior he chooses."

Her brother's troubling words stayed in her mind the next day as she paddled away. She was cheered, however, by the sight of Jamestown, where she decided to put in and stay for a few days.

She found John-Smith in the shade of the lookout tower, making marks with his writing feather in the little book he called his journal. His face looked burned by the sun.

"Little Sister!" he shouted in greeting. "I have adventures to tell you about!" He rolled up his sleeve to show her a fresh ugly scar on his arm.

"What happened?" she asked.

"Percy and I went exploring up the coastline in the boat we built. We met other tribes — the Rappahannocks and the Susquehanna. They took us spear-fishing in their river. We caught something huge, and when I reached out to grab it, it stung me with its tail. It was a stingray!"

Pocahontas clapped her hand to her mouth in horror. She had heard about this monster fish.

"I thought I would die for sure," he went on. "My arm swelled up and turned purple. It burned like fire. I told the men to dig my grave, and I laid down beside it. But then the fever went away. They carried me back to the boat to rest. And that night, I ate some of that blasted fish!" He roared with laughter, and Pocahontas laughed with him.

The next day Captain Newport's ship returned from his fast voyage to England and back. Pocahontas clung happily to her half-brother Namontack, and showered him with questions. He was overflowing with strange wonders to report from the land of the white men.

Captain Newport also brought with him the first white women Pocahontas had ever seen. She was amazed to discover that what John-Smith told her was true: The English women wore skirts that were wider at the bottom than a doorway! Pocahontas made friends with the women, and also with a new boy named Henry. Henry's yellow hair was so light it was nearly white. He was quiet and shy, but with only two cartwheels on the riverbank, Pocahontas got Henry to smile and talk.

That night she was among several guests from Jamestown for dinner with Captain Newport aboard the ship. He seemed astonished at how much English she had learned during his time away.

After the meal he brought out a paper from his pocket, and gave it to John-Smith. Elder Brother scowled as he read it. He threw the paper down. Pocahontas wondered what this troubling message could be.

"It can only cause more harm than good!" John-Smith grumbled.

"I'm afraid you're right," Captain Newport answered calmly. "But it's our duty."

He looked at Pocahontas. "My child, we have a message for you to take home with you. The king of England has sent us gifts for your father. And the king of England wishes to honor Chief Powhatan by having him crowned King of All the Chesapeake."

"It's a foolish idea!" John-Smith shouted, as he pounded the table with his fist. Pocahontas thought Chief Powhatan would agree.

On a stormy morning eight days later, Pocahontas was with her father and his leading warriors in the council longhouse at Comoco. A runner, wet from the rain, arrived with news: The English were on their way from Jamestown for the crowning ceremony.

Ever since Pocahontas had faithfully delivered her message from England's king, the same question was asked again and again by everyone here: How could Powhatan be crowned king when he was already the king?

The wind-blown rain pounded on the longhouse roof. This was the season when the Destroying Wind often blew in from the Great Gray Ocean, bringing the worst storms of the year. Around the village, any bark and hide coverings that were loose had already blown away from the wigwams. Tree limbs were snapping and crashing in the forest.

"I don't think the Bearded Ones will make it here," Tatacoope predicted. "Surely this storm will be the end of them, and of their village."

That afternoon the wind grew weaker. The next day the English appeared, some on the forest trail, and others on Captain Newport's ship that had sailed up the river. While still wondering about the meaning of the ceremony, Pocahontas and everyone in Comoco offered hospitality to their guests. Pocahontas served plums and roasted pumpkin seeds to her friends.

The great ceremony began when an English soldier blew into a shiny metal horn called a trumpet. The bellowing noise it made brought everyone together just outside the council longhouse.

Captain Newport's men carried forward their biggest gift for Chief Powhatan: a bed like the ones Pocahontas had seen in the houses of Jamestown. But this one had curtains laced with golden thread, and the frame was made of shiny carved wood. Pocahontas knew the mattress was probably filled with feathers. As the bed was carried by, one of her younger half-brothers jumped on the mattress and bounced. This brought laughter from English and Algonquins alike. Pocahontas wanted to bounce too, but she remembered her dignity as a princess.

Then Captain Newport brought forward a long purple cape. "This belonged to King James himself," he said.

Pocahontas translated this information into Algonquin for her father. But he said nothing as the garment was draped around his shoulders by Captain Newport.

More soldiers stepped forward before Powhatan. One of them carried a purple velvet cloth folded on his hands. Resting on the cloth was a silver crown. Captain Newport picked up the crown, and two of his soldiers moved close to stand beside Chief Powhatan and his daughter.

Captain Newport held out the crown. He said to Pocahontas, "Tell your father now that he may kneel."

She passed along the message to her father. He looked at her in disgust. "I have never bent my knee to any man," he growled.

"Perhaps, Father, just this once, you could do it."

"No," he thundered.

Pocahontas saw impatience building on the faces of the soldiers standing beside them.

"These white men are not as tall as you," she said to Powhatan. "Could you tilt forward your head just a little, Father, so they can put the crown on easier?"

"But I care nothing for this crown," he answered. "I am already the mighty Powhatan, ruler of the Chesapeake!"

Suddenly one of the soldiers grabbed the chief's shoulders from behind, and leaned his head forward. Captain Newport quickly popped on the crown.

Pocahontas stepped back in fear. Not even his own warriors would ever dare lay hands on such a great king! But before her father had time to respond, another white soldier waved a banner. With that signal, a blast of thunder sounded from a cannon on the ship.

Powhatan jumped as if he had been shot. But when he saw that no was hurt, he set his jaw, squared his shoulders, and regained his dignity. His face was sober and scowling, but he said nothing.

Pocahontas breathed a sigh. At last, the awkward ceremony was over.

As the English left to go home, Pocahontas promised John-

Smith that she would soon visit Jamestown again. "And the cold of winter is not far away," she added. "When it comes, I too will come to see how you are, as often as I can."

Before nightfall she was summoned into the council long-house. Her father sat on his throne. His face still wore the stony expression she had seen when the ceremony ended.

She stood before him.

"Pocahontas," he said soberly, "you will go no more to visit the village of the Bearded Ones. They are foolish men who do foolish things.

"My daughter, you are no longer a child, and you may no longer run about carefree as a child. There are new things you must learn and do now. You will have no more time for the white men.

"I forbid you from going to the Tassen-tassees ever again. If you go to them, I will see it as betrayal. If you disobey me in this, I will banish you from my presence forever."

CHAPTER THIRTEEN

TERROR AT NIGHT

THE DESTROYING WIND blew twice more that fall, for several days each time. The winds and rain were worse than anyone could remember. Silently, Pocahontas wondered how well Jamestown had endured.

The Quiyow danced and wailed through the village. Okewas was angry, he said. This was the reason for the storms.

On one cold and windy day, Tatacoope returned on the forest trail. More sailing ships had been sighted at Jamestown, he reported. The Bearded Ones were becoming stronger. Pocahontas let no one see how glad she was to hear this news.

But that night in the council longhouse, she heard the Quiyow screeching out his warning: If the Bearded Ones were not driven away soon, Okewas would demand more sacrifices to the Dark Magic. His words chilled her heart even more than the Wolf Wind that swirled in the darkness outside.

As the winter deepened, Pocahontas heard more reports from her father's spies. At villages all around the Chesapeake, the Bearded Ones were visiting and seeking trade. But Chief Powhatan had now forbidden any dealings with the Tassen-tassees.

In one village the people had accepted copper and beads from John-Smith and his men, but had given no corn in return. So Nantaquod set fire to one of their longhouses.

Elder Brother seemed to be growing desperate, Pocahontas thought. She longed to be able to take something to all her friends at Jamestown.

One morning she saw her father giving instructions to Thomas, the white boy sent by Captain Newport to serve Chief Powhatan. Thomas was wrapped in a rabbit-fur cloak. He nodded to her father, and walked out of the village.

Three days later she and Kahnessa were tending a cooking fire, staying close to its warmth. They were huddled together beneath fur blankets. Pocahontas could not remember having such cold weather so early in winter. Even the river was filling up with ice. She was glad the Quiyow was not dancing and wailing around, blaming the cold on the Bearded Ones.

She looked up from the fire and saw Thomas returning. With him were several Bearded Ones. They were carrying tools, long pieces of wood, and even window-glass.

She left the comfort of the fire and stepped over to Thomas. "What is all this?" she asked him.

Thomas answered that he had been to Jamestown with a message. Chief Powhatan was now ready to trade. He wanted the Bearded Ones to build him an English house here in Comoco. When the new house was built, he promised to give them a barge-load of corn.

"So Captain Smith will soon be on his way upriver with the barge," Thomas added, before running along to give his report to Chief Powhatan.

Pocahontas tried to relax the knot of worry that was forming in her stomach.

She watched the next two days as the white men worked on
the house. As it took shape, she did not think it looked as fine as
the houses in Jamestown. But she hoped her father would be
pleased.

The next morning, the barge was sighted in the middle of
the ice-choked river. It appeared to be stuck. The villagers lined
the riverbank to watch. Soon they saw Bearded Ones making
their way on foot to shore, sometimes wading in chest-deep
water, and sometimes walking on pieces of ice.

The villagers built a shelter of poles and branches for the
shivering men by the river, with a fire inside, plus a supply of
meat. In strict obedience to her father's command, Pocahontas
stayed away from her friends.

When darkness fell, Chief Powhatan called for his favorite
daughter. He asked Pocahontas to go to the shelter and invite
John-Smith to meet with him in the council longhouse. He
asked Pocahontas to be present in the meeting as well, but not
to say anything.

As she turned to go, Powhatan called her name.

"Yes, Father?"

"It is only this once that I allow you to go to the Tassen-
tassees. You may not do so ever again. Do you understand?"

"I do, Father."

Pocahontas walked down to the shelter. In silence, she
brought John-Smith back with her.

Chief Powhatan began the meeting with a surprising question to Nantaquod: "Why have you come to us?"

"I have come because you sent for me," Elder Brother

answered. "My men are building you an English house, and now we've brought our barge to take back the corn you promised in exchange."

Powhatan laughed. "I made no such offer. If you want our corn, you must pay for it. One sword or one gun for every basketful of corn."

John-Smith's face was turning red. "Great Chief," he said, "I have told you that I have no swords or guns to spare."

"Each man of you has a sword or gun," Powhatan argued. "I can no longer allow you to carry these in Comoco. You must give them to me now."

John-Smith's voice was rising. "But I never ask your braves to hand over their bows and arrows and spears when they come to Jamestown!"

"Give the weapons to me," Powhatan demanded, "or else you must all return tonight across the ice to your boat."

Pocahontas was sure John-Smith would never give in to these demands. Yet she was also sure her father knew this. Why was Powhatan continuing this argument? What was he trying to do?

Her father stood up. "I will loan you a little corn tomorrow," he announced. "But you will owe me for it." Before John-Smith could answer, her father stepped from his throne and walked out of the longhouse.

In her wigwam all that night, Pocahontas did not sleep. She could not chase away her concern for the safety of her friends. But what could she do for them?

The next morning she wrapped fox-fur around her. She climbed a tree high on the bank upriver from the village, to watch. But nothing seemed to be happening. The white men stayed in the warmth of their shelter, and her own people stayed inside the village. She was so tired that her eyes closed in sleep a few times.

Not until late in the afternoon did she see Powhatan's warriors taking basketfuls of corn down to the men in the shelter. The warriors did not offer to help load them on the barge. She watched as the white men began carrying the baskets across the ice and water to the boat. But night was falling again long before the job was finished. She saw the half-wet men building another big fire at their shelter by the river. It looked as if the Bearded Ones would spend another night there.

"Pocahontas!"

She looked down from her tree. It was already so dark she could hardly recognize Namontack on the ground below. It was he who had whispered her name. She hurried down. He spoke to her quietly, and in English.

"The Bearded Ones are in great danger!"

"I was afraid so," she whispered. "Do you know Father's plan?"

"Yes. I heard only a little, while he was talking to Tatacoope. Later tonight, when the darkness is deep, they'll take meat to the shelter. When the Bearded Ones have laid down their weapons and are busy eating, our warriors will attack."

Pocahontas looked once more toward the shelter that she had been watching all day. Through spaces between the poles and branches, she could see the warming fire inside.

She could stay away no longer.

"I will warn them," she told Namontack. "Go at once and tell Kahnessa what I'm doing. The two of you can watch for me, while I'm slipping along the riverbank to the shelter. Go and talk with her by the village gate. If you see anything that might be danger for me—if the warriors with the food are on their way before I've come back to you—then Kahnessa must laugh at something you say. She must laugh loudly so I can hear her down at the river."

With her plan in place, Pocahontas set out at once. From inside the village she heard the happy voices of her people as they lifted cooked food off their firepits. She heard the voices of the Bearded Ones and the crackling of their fire from inside the shelter. She heard her own heartbeats, pounding like a drum. But her moccasined feet were silent. And she heard no laughter in the familiar voice of Kahnessa.

She was nearly breathless as she slipped into the shelter, and saw the surprised faces of the white men. On the far side she quickly spotted John-Smith, seated with the others around the fire. At once the men became quiet enough to hear her whisper.

"My father plans to bring food tonight and kill you while you eat. You must go. Now!"

John-Smith rushed to her side. "Little Princess," he said, "surely you've risked your life to come warn us. How can I thank you?"

His eyes filled with tears. He reached to his neck and lifted over his head the string that held the compass.

"No, Elder Brother. I dare not be seen with anything that is yours." She knew tears were streaming down her cheeks, but she did not care that all these men saw her weeping.

"Elder Brother," she cried. "I fear I will never see you again!"

She forced herself to turn and go out of the shelter. She returned carefully and slowly along the riverbank.

Moments later, she let Kahnessa and Namontack see her as she made her way through the village to the wigwam. She lay on her sleeping mat, and covered herself with the fox-fur that had kept her warm all day in the tree.

Mother came in with her little brother. She offered Pocahontas food, but she could not eat. Kahnessa came in as well. Soon everyone, even Kahnessa, was asleep.

But Pocahontas listened. She waited, and listened.

How long would it take before she could be sure the Bearded Ones were safe? Would her father's warriors go after them when they found the shelter empty? Would Elder Brother and his men be able to unlock their barge from the ice, and get away?

She had never felt this tired before, but still she could not sleep.

Then, for the second time since the sun last went down, she heard her name whispered: "Pocahontas!"

Filled with fear she hurried out of the wigwam. It was the white boy Thomas. He motioned for her to follow.

Her uncertainty was crushing her, but they walked on in silence. Finally she and Thomas were outside the village. There stood Remcoe. Beside him was a Bearded One whom she did not know.

"I took the west watch tonight," Remcoe said. "I wanted no part of the attack on the Tassen-tassees. But now this Bearded One has come on the forest trail, and is asking for John-Smith. Kahnessa already told me what you did. So I wouldn't let him go inside the village. What should we do with him?"

Pocahontas turned to the white man. "Who are you?" she said in English. "Why are you here?"

"Richard Wiffin," he answered. "We've had an accident in Jamestown. One of our fishing boats sank, and we lost eleven men. I came to tell Captain Smith, so he wouldn't linger here."

"He hasn't," Pocahontas answered. "He's on his way back to Jamestown tonight, on the barge." Speaking aloud those words filled Pocahontas with confidence and calmness. Yes, surely Elder Brother was safe now.

"And you're in danger if you don't leave also," she told the Bearded One.

"Remcoe, start him back on the trail. And Thomas, hurry over to the guard on the east watch. Tell him you heard noises in that direction, so he'll go the wrong way."

No more was said as the others left Pocahontas alone.

She looked up. A half-moon had risen. She prayed, "O Creator God, let this moonlight show the way home for John-Smith and his men in the barge, and for the Bearded One on the forest trail."

Back in her wigwam and ready to sleep at last, the Princess thought how strongly she had set her spirit against her father's will tonight. Would he ever know?

Both she and Kahnessa slept later than usual the next morning. They walked together to the river to dip beneath floating bits of ice. They wrapped their shivering bodies in fur cloaks. The morning air was sharp and cold, but the sky was clear and the sun promised warmth. They sat for a while and let it shine on them before they slowly walked back.

In the village they were surprised to see a group of women surrounding their wigwam. They pressed through the circle. Tatacoope was taking out Halewa's few belongings and throwing them on the ground.

"What are you doing?" Kahnessa shouted.

"Our father has sent Halewa away," Tatacoope sneered. "She

and her boy-child are being taken by canoe to Potomac, the village where she came from. They've already gone."

Pocahontas and Kahnessa looked at each other with stricken eyes.

"Your mother doesn't belong in the same village as mighty Powhatan and his proud warriors," Tatacoope continued. "Her people have always been weak and mild."

As he stomped away, he looked back at Pocahontas. "And it must be her blood that gives you such a weakness for stinking Tassen-tassees — and stupid otters!"

The circle of women drifted away to leave Kahnessa and Pocahontas alone. The two girls rushed inside the wigwam, and sobbed on their sleeping mats.

"He sent her away because of me," Pocahontas declared. "Father knows what I've done. But he can't prove it. So he banished Halewa instead of me."

In the days that followed, while everyone was preparing for the winter trip to the hunting camp, the other villagers spoke only the most necessary words to Pocahontas. No one said anything to her about her mother.

Chief Powhatan never even looked in her direction. Pocahontas could feel his anger. It was cold anger, as cold as the winter nights when she and Kahnessa huddled alone in their wigwam.

On the day the villagers were to leave for the hunting camp, her father sent Thomas to her with this message: "You are not to come to the hunting camp. You are to remain behind with the very old and the very young."

She watched silently as the others — Remcoe and Kahnessa, and Namontack, and Nanoon and Kewelah, and the rest — walked away on the trail to the Blue-Haze Mountains. She promised herself that she would endure this test. "If I only stay strong," she said, "then someday Father's anger will pass. Someday he'll smile at me again."

CHAPTER FOURTEEN

ESCAPE

POCAHONTAS ENDURED the loneliness as winter's coldest days went by. One day the villagers returned from the hunting camp.

After the return, her father did not speak to the Princess often, but at least she did not feel such coldness in his anger.

Spring came, and the Planting Song was sung, though this time Pocahontas did not hear Halewa singing it. Summer came, and the Berry-picking Song was sung, but Pocahontas did not awaken to hear her mother humming it.

Parahunt returned for a visit that summer. As chief of another village now, he was given a feast of welcome at Comoco. He took a walk with Pocahontas along the river. He had visited Halewa, and he told Pocahontas that their mother was doing well. So was Little Otter, he added. Parahunt also told her that Nantaquod was building a log house and was clearing land near Parahunt's village.

"And I have other news: Father has made a choice about your future husband."

Pocahontas felt a lump in her throat. She struggled to say, "And who is this man of my father's choosing?"

"He's a warrior you don't know. His name is Kokum, from the Paspeg tribe of our Uncle Opech. He's a man of great courage. He fought well in our raids against the Iroquois. Yes, he's strong in spirit — maybe even strong enough to stand up to you!" Parahunt chuckled at his own comment, but Pocahontas hoped her brother noticed that she wasn't laughing.

His voice grew more gentle. "Surely Father will let you meet him soon."

"Chief Powhatan's anger must still be very great," she answered coldly, "if he will not talk with his daughter about her own engagement."

Parahunt said nothing more about it.

One fall morning, when the trees of the forest wore their brightest yellows and reds, Pocahontas was outside her wigwam cutting long, thin strips of deermeat. The deer had wandered close to the village, and Remcoe had shot it with his bow. After cutting the strips, Pocahontas would salt and dry them to provide food for the winter. This was work she had always done before with Halewa, and she thought of her mother often this morning.

She heard young voices speaking English, and looked up in surprise. Thomas was talking with Henry, the white-haired boy she had met in Jamestown.

"Henry, what are you doing here?" she asked.

"Spending time with Thomas, before the others get here," he answered.

"What others?"

"The men from Jamestown, in the barges. They're bringing copper and cloth to trade for the corn that Powhatan promised."

"But when did my father make such a promise?"

Thomas answered this time. "I took the message to

Jamestown last week. Chief Powhatan says he's ready to trade now."

"But John-Smith would never let his men try that again, not after they were tricked last time."

"Oh, haven't you heard?" Henry asked. "Captain Smith is no longer there. He's gone back to England."

"To England! Why?"

"He got hurt in a gunpowder explosion. Bad burns all over his arm."

The boys ran along, after Thomas said he would show Henry more of the village.

Pocahontas left her work. She rushed out to her special place by the river, and sat down. "Oh, Creator God," she prayed, "help John-Smith. Help him not to hurt anymore."

Then her own hurt made her burst into sobs. Why did so many of those she loved have to be taken far away?

But there was no use asking that question. It would not bring Halewa back, or Little Otter, or Elder Brother. Instead, she forced herself to think. With Elder Brother gone from Jamestown, the Tassen-tassees might act with great foolishness. Perhaps her father knew John-Smith wasn't there, and he was setting the same trap for the Bearded Ones that he had tried only last winter.

She must go back to the village and watch carefully, and be ready to do whatever she could.

She prayed for the Creator God to make her strong.

The next day, her worst nightmares became real. She awoke to the sound of war drums. All morning she saw the Quiyow strutting and prancing in the village as he wailed. She saw Thomas and Henry thrown inside a wigwam and kept there.

Powhatan's warriors put on their warpaint and called out their war cries. Warriors from other villages arrived to join them in the coming battle.

As the drums and the wailing and the war songs sounded in her ears, the dreadful fear inside Pocahontas began to turn to anger. She was angry at her father, and angry at Okewas the War God and at all who served him. Because of them, the river would soon be red with blood.

She could not bear to watch it happen. But there was no way she could fight it. All she could do was run away.

The drums and dances grew wilder after sunset. She and Kahnessa were alone in their wigwam, with the sounds of coming war pounding in their ears. When the darkness was full, Pocahontas began throwing a few belongings in a basket.

"What are you doing?" Kahnessa asked.

"I go to see our Mother. I'll live with her people at Potomac. I can stay here no longer."

"I understand," Kahnessa said. "But I must stay with Remcoe."

The two sisters embraced, then Pocahontas stepped out. In the darkness of the moonless night, she quickly slipped away from the village that had always been her home. She went north, in the opposite direction from Jamestown.

Five sunsets later, Pocohontas was helping grind corn beside her mother's wigwam in Potomac. Pocahontas looked up from the grinding stone, where both she and her mother were kneeling. She saw Parahunt.

Pocahontas stood. Her brother came close, and clasped her shoulders in greeting.

"Kahnessa told me you were here, Little Sister."

He said no more, so she quietly asked, "What news do you have of the battle?"

Parahunt answered gravely. "Two full boats of the Bearded Ones came up the river from Jamestown, expecting to trade. Our father's trap was ready for them. Only a few of our people were killed. But of the Tassen-tassees, sixty scalps were taken."

Pocahontas closed her eyes, and her legs went weak. Sixty scalps! Never had she heard of a battle where so many were killed. And she was sure that never had she known so many of the dead. These were men whom she had taught to plant corn, and given herbs when they were ill.

"Only one English man escaped," Parahunt added. "And one young boy was taken captive."

"What will we be done with the child?" Pocahontas asked.

"I don't know. For now he's with two other white boys who were already in the village."

Halewa was still kneeling at the grinding stone. "Perhaps it will not be good for the three boys," she said, as she slowly stood up. "There will be more battles now. And for more battles, Oke-was will demand more sacrifices." She shook her head, and walked into her wigwam.

"Come, my sister," Parahunt said. Sorrow made Pocahontas feel weary, but she followed her brother. Near the village gate, Parahunt whistled to one of his warriors who had come with him. The man picked up a basket and brought it closer and laid it at her feet.

"Little Sister," Parahunt announced, "a good friend wishes to honor you." He reached down and pulled back the basket lid. Out jumped a familiar shining head.

"Little Otter!" she cried. He wiggled into her arms and barked a happy greeting.

Parahunt laughed and said to his sister, "Your new home can be his new home."

The next night Pocahontas was alone with Little Otter, watching him play in the third river-home of his short life. It was good to have him near her again, this creature who seemed so like her in spirit. She must learn to be more like him, she decided. Never tired and never fearful. Quick and bold.

Parahunt had gone away this morning. But her mind kept hearing the news he had brought about the three white boys held in Comoco, and the warning her mother had sounded.

"I've decided to do something," she called to her pet as he swam in loops on the surface. "To do it, I must be tireless and fearless like you, and quick and bold.

"Little Otter, I know three boys who would love to play with you. I want to bring them back here to live with us. Do you think I should try to do this?"

Little Otter swam toward her, with his nose in the air. He gave a quick bark.

And that meant yes, Pocahontas decided.

Several days later, Pocahontas joined a parade of twenty warriors and maidens carrying food from Potomac to Comoco. It was time for the yearly presentation of food gifts from all the outlying villages to Chief Powhatan.

As they came into Comoco, Pocahontas broke away from her new tribesmen and ran to greet Kahnessa with an embrace and kisses. Remcoe soon joined them.

"Our wedding day has been set by the village's wise women,"

he told Pocahontas. "Kahnessa will be my wife before the new moon. Can you stay here with us until after the wedding?"

Before she could answer, a shadow seemed to fall over them. They turned and saw the Quiyow standing and staring at them, only three paces away. Pocahontas drew back her arms from her sister. She thought the Spirit Man looked more bent and shriveled and ugly than ever. His narrow eyes were on the same level as hers.

For the first time in her life, he spoke directly to Pocahontas. "Why do you come here?"

She answered loudly, so everyone around could hear. "I have come with the food taxes from Potomac. And is it not right that I come to wish my sister well? For the day of her marriage is approaching."

The Quiyow narrowed his eyes even more. He turned and walked away.

The next night Kahnessa and Pocahontas were together with the three white boys. They shared a meal of squirrel meat and corncakes. Besides Thomas and white-headed Henry, there was also Samuel. He and Thomas were the first two boys Pocahontas met long ago in Jamestown. Samuel was still showing the shock of the attack he had witnessed. He could hardly answer Pocahontas, even when she spoke gently and slowly.

"Are any of you afraid?" she asked the boys.

"Yes," Henry said. "We don't know what will happen to us if this war keeps going."

"Tomorrow," Pocahontas said, "I'm going back to my new home in Potomac. I have a pet otter there. If you want to, you can come with me tomorrow and visit. You can even live there, if you decide you like it."

Samuel managed a weak smile. "I've never seen an otter," he said.

In the morning, the three English boys fell in line with Pocahontas and the Potomac people as they prepared to leave.

At the edge of the village, the old Spirit Man appeared again. His arms were crossed, and live snakes were hanging again from his ears. He took a stand in the pathway.

Again he spoke to Pocahontas. "Where are these white boys going?" he demanded.

"To visit me in Potomac." Pocahontas kept her voice even. "I've told them about my pet otter, and they want to go and see him."

The Quiyow's eyes flared at her. But he took one step back from the path, and let them all go by.

As they traveled, Pocahontas and the boys stayed at the rear of the group. She kept looking back. They had not gone far when she felt a tug at her deerskin sleeve.

It was Henry.

"Thomas has turned back!" he said.

How could it be? Again she looked on the trail behind them. Thomas was nowhere in sight. But it was too dangerous to go back and get him now.

"Yes," she said to Henry, "he must have gone back because he's lived at Comoco so long, and doesn't want to leave. Or perhaps he forgot something, and he'll catch up with us later. Let's keep walking!"

As they moved ahead, she whispered to Henry and Samuel. "If anything should happen, if something goes wrong, make sure you run forward, and not back to Comoco."

The words were barely out of her mouth when a chilling yell

echoed through the forest. The Quiyow jumped onto the trail behind them. With him were two young priests of the War God. They were screaming and waving tomahawks and knives. The Potomac people who were with Pocahontas stepped back from the trail. They would not dare to oppose the priests of Okewas.

Pocahontas pushed Henry and Samuel forward. Henry raced into the woods and was quickly out of sight. Samuel ran along the trail screaming, but one of the young priests came after him. He threw his tomahawk. Samuel's scream stopped at once, and the boy fell dead in the path.

Then the Quiyow and the two priests disappeared, back into the shadows.

Pocahontas could only cry out in rage.

It was nearly evening before she found Henry in the forest. He was lying dazed and shivering behind a fallen log. She took him by the hand and lifted him up. "Come with me," she told him. "I promise you'll be safe." She wrapped her arms around him, to calm and warm him before taking him on to Potomac.

And she vowed silently that she would never let herself be that close to the old Spirit Man again.

CHAPTER FIFTEEN

TAKEN AWAY

WRAPPING BOTH ARMS around the smooth-barked maple tree, Pocahontas stared out across the river. Here, after all this time, a Swan Boat had come to her quiet village of Potomac. What could it mean?

She had not seen one of these ships in many moons. In more than three years she had not seen a single Bearded One, and it seemed an eternity since she had helped the white men escape from Comoco on that cold night when she said goodbye to Elder Brother in the riverside shelter, and saw the warming fire reflected in his tears.

The only white face she had seen at all in these last three years was Henry's — grinning, white-haired Henry, who still lived here at Potomac. Henry had become one of her favorite companions, along with Mother Halewa, and Little Otter, and also the grayhound Kint, whom her father had sent to her as a gift.

Chief Powhatan was someone else she had not seen in three years. Even if she returned to visit in Comoco, she still would not see him there. He had moved far away to the village of Rassa-wack, and made it his capital.

This was the news she heard from Parahunt, who visited often in Potomac. He told her of the fighting that continued with the Bearded Ones. Kokum, the warrior whom her father had chosen for her to marry, had been killed in one of the bat-tles. So had Tatacoope and Namontack.

Parahunt was astonished at how powerful the white people had become. Many Algonquin villages and fields had been burned and the people driven from their homes. It seemed that the English no longer needed to trade for Algonquin corn. What they wanted most was more land. They had started many new villages of their own, and planted many new fields.

Pocahontas pressed her cheek against the smooth maple bark. She had seemed so far away from all these big changes that Parahunt talked about. Could big changes be coming here to Potomac as well?

She heard someone behind her coming from the village. She unlocked her arms around the tree, and looked back. It was Jopassus, a young warrior who was marked out to be chief some-day of the Potomac people.

"Pocahontas," he called, "I have something to ask of you."

"What is it, Jopassus?"

He pointed across the water to the Swan Boat. "The leader of the Tassen-tassee ship has asked me to visit him. My wife wants very much to go, too. But she is afraid to be on the ship without another woman. Pocahontas, will you come with us?"

Pocahontas looked out at the ship again. Perhaps it would be unwise to have anything more to do with the ways of white men. Perhaps it could only bring her more sadness.

Jopassus spoke again. "Surely you wouldn't be afraid! You've already seen all the strange and wonderful things the Tassentassees have. You know all about them. Will you come with us, Pocahontas, so my wife will not be fearful?"

It would indeed be good, Pocahontas thought, if there was less fear of one another between the Algonquins and the Bearded Ones. If there was less fear, maybe there would be less fighting.

"Yes, Jopassus. To make it easier for your wife, I will go — but only for a short visit."

Later that morning, as they were being taken out to the ship in a rowboat, Pocahontas had fresh doubts about whether she should have come. For one thing, Jopassus's wife did not seem at all fearful.

When they were helped out of the boat onto the big ship, a tall man introduced himself as Captain Argall. He wore a hat with a strange feather on it. He took off his hat and bowed to kiss her hand.

"Princess Pocahontas," he said loudly, "you honor us with your presence!"

He led her to a room where he offered her a glass of what he called "the finest of wines." Pocahontas wondered where Jopassus and his wife had wandered to on the ship.

"You've truly become a lovely lady," Captain Argall said, "since the days of your girlhood when you served our people so well at Jamestown." He began mentioning the people in Jamestown who remembered her service to them.

Suddenly Pocahontas felt a motion that frightened her. It was not the gentle swaying that she remembered on Captain Newport's ship. No — they were moving!

She ran to the small window in the room. Yes, the village and the riverbank were slipping away. The ship was really moving! "Where are we going?" she cried.

"Pocahontas, I must take you back to Jamestown," Captain Argall said. "But you need not fear me. I won't treat you as a prisoner, but as my honored guest."

She screamed, "Jopassus!"

"He can't hear you," Captain Argall said. "He and his wife have gone back to the village. It was they who agreed to bring you into my care."

Pocahontas was struggling to understand. "But why? Why would they betray me?"

"I bought their help," Captain Argall answered. "With a copper kettle."

"No!" Pocahontas shouted in unbelief.

Captain Argall made his way for the door. "I'll return in a moment with food for you." He shut the door behind him.

Pocahontas looked out the window again. The village was quickly growing smaller. Then her eyes caught a silver streak on the riverbank. She looked closer. It was Kint! And behind him, struggling to keep up, was Henry. At least her friend had seen what happened to her.

Captain Argall soon returned with bread and fruit, but she would eat nothing.

"Please, Princess," he said, "I mean you no harm. Please eat!"

"How do I know you mean me no harm? What will be done with me?"

"Pocahontas, you truly have nothing to fear. In Jamestown you'll meet with the Governor, and then you'll be taken to a place not far from there called Henrico. You'll stay on a farm and be cared for by a good man, Reverend Whitaker, and his wife. They are kind and gentle. Everything you need will be provided."

"But everything I need is already mine in Potomac," she responded. "So why should I be taken anywhere else? What are you trying to do?"

"I am trying to bring peace. For too long the Algonquins have waged war against us—"

She interrupted him. "What can you expect? You're driving the tribes from their land!"

"We drive them away because we fear them," he answered. "But this need not be. Too many lives are being lost on both sides. I've taken you captive in the hopes that your father will release the English prisoners he has, and that he will return our stolen guns. He must listen to us, if we hold his favorite daughter in our keeping.

"The Governor at Jamestown and I have agreed to this plan to try to win peace. We have never wanted war. As you know, peace has always been our people's true desire, going all the way back to the beginning, to the days of your friend, Captain Smith."

At the mention of Elder Brother's name, she could not hold back a question. "What news is there of my friend?"

Captain Argall paused before he answered. "Some say there was word from England that he is dead, but I gather it's only a rumor. There may be no truth to it. I just don't know. Pocahontas, I do request that you eat something, please."

She made no answer. Captain Argall left the room. Pocahontas felt a darkness weighing down upon her, and she sank to the floor.

As they neared Jamestown, she was allowed to come up on

the ship's deck. She was amazed to see a crowd of people on the riverbank outside the village. She heard shouts: "God bless the Princess! Three cheers for Pocahontas!"

"See, you are loved here," Captain Argall said. "Everyone knows about your kindness."

She was speechless as she stepped onto the new dock at the Jamestown riverbank. She was led through the cheering crowd and taken inside the largest building in the village.

The man they called the Governor was there, with other leaders of Jamestown. Almost all of them were new faces to her.

"Princess Pocahontas," the Governor said, "we have already sent news of your presence with us to Chief Powhatan. We have demanded that Chief Powhatan give us back our men whom he has captured, and our guns and ammunition that he has stolen. We have also asked for peace between our peoples. Our hope is that your father, out of love for his daughter as well as his own desire for peace, will agree to our demands."

The Governor and all the men in the room looked to Pocahontas for a reply.

"I am sure my father will think carefully about what you say," she said. "But no one can demand anything from the great Powhatan. He will do what he will do."

CHAPTER SIXTEEN

READY

AT HENRICO the days went by slowly for Pocahontas, with no word of Powhatan's response to the English demands.

Meanwhile she soon felt at ease with Reverend Whitaker and his wife. They spoke gently, and they seemed wise. Reverend Whitaker reminded her of Reverend Hunt, and of the unfinished story he left with her before he died — the story of the man Jesus, the Son of the Creator God.

It was the kindness of the Whitakers that kept Pocahontas there. She had already seen how easy it would be to slip away. She was sure that at night she could sneak past the English soldiers posted around the farm, and go back to Potomac.

The Whitakers' house was the finest she had ever seen. It was made of a stone they called brick. The house was filled with things Pocahontas never saw in the roughly built houses of Jamestown's early days. In a room called the kitchen, Mrs. Whitaker showed Pocahontas how she cooked and how she sewed. Pocahontas helped her. She was amazed at the tiny metal needles Mrs. Whitaker used.

One morning — on the sixth day after she arrived in Henrico

— Pocahontas was sitting in the kitchen practicing her sewing on some scrap cloth. Mrs. Whitaker stepped into the room and said, "Pocahontas, dear, you have a visitor at the front door."

Pocahontas set aside the needle and thread and cloth, and walked through the house. In the open front doorway, Parahunt was standing.

She ran to embrace him.

"You look well, Little Sister," he said. He seemed surprised that this was so.

"Yes," she assured him. "I'm well."

Parahunt held her at arm's length, with his hands resting on her shoulders. "I've come to tell you our father's answer to the English. A runner is going even now to Jamestown to give the message to the white chief there. But I myself wanted to let you know. Father has released the captive Bearded Ones that he was holding at Rassa-wack. And for now, he has put a stop to all the fighting."

Pocahontas closed her eyes and offered a silent prayer of thanksgiving to the Creator God.

Parahunt continued: "It was hard for Father to give up the prisoners, as you can understand. And he has completely refused to meet the other demand. He will not send back any of the weapons.

"But I must tell you, Little Sister, that Father's heart aches for you. When the runner came with the news of your capture, he grieved. He stayed in the council longhouse and spoke not a word for three days. Uncle Opech wanted to gather every warrior and destroy Jamestown, but Powhatan was afraid the foolish Bearded Ones would panic, and harm you."

Parahunt took her hands in his own. "Father wanted me to

say to you that, in his old age, you are still his Pocahontas. You're still his Favorite Daughter. And he longs to know that you are safe."

Pocahontas felt her tears coming. "Tell Father I'm very safe. Tell him, my Brother, that you've seen this with your own eyes."

"If he knows you aren't in danger," Parahunt said, "then we won't see more fighting for a while. Father will simply wait on the English."

"If that's true," Pocahontas answered, "perhaps it's better for me to be here than anywhere else."

She sadly watched Parahunt leave. And she told herself, *If Father can wait, then so can I.*

The Whitakers had a little table which they used just for writing. They let Pocahontas sit there whenever she wanted, and gave her ink and paper. She even had her own feather-pen. She learned to make the English letters that Elder Brother had shown her years before.

"White Feather is my spirit-name," she told Reverend Whitaker one day as she was using the feather-pen to write all twenty-six letters. "I have other names too." Reverend Whitaker showed her how to write each of her names using the letters. He also praised her for how fast she learned.

"My mother used to tell me," Pocahontas said, "that my mind was like a large basket, finely woven. It holds everything that's put into it."

In the evenings by candlelight, Reverend Whitaker read aloud to her from the Bible. Each night Pocahontas asked him to keep reading more. And each night, sometimes after hours of reading, Reverend Whitaker would say with a yawn that he just had to go to bed, and that tomorrow he would start again where he had stopped.

Reverend Whitaker taught her a prayer to the Creator God in heaven. It began by calling God "Our Father." Pocahontas loved the prayer, because she had never thought of God before as her Father. Reverend Whitaker said the prayer was written in the Bible, and that it came from Jesus, God's Son, who makes it possible for us to know God as our Father.

She also quickly learned what Reverend Whitaker called the Creed. It began, "I believe in God the Father Almighty, maker of heaven and earth, and in Jesus Christ His only Son our Lord..." The Creed went on to say that after Jesus died, He rose up from the dead on the third day. *So this,* Pocahontas thought, *is the rest of the story that Reverend Hunt wanted me to hear.*

She began asking Reverend Whitaker all the questions she had not been able to ask Reverend Hunt before he died.

Mrs. Whitaker gave Pocahontas dresses to wear. At first she was annoyed by how noisy they were, no matter how quietly she tried to walk. "These dresses are meant to rustle," Mrs. Whitaker explained. "The rustling sound tells everyone that a lady has entered the room."

One day Pocahontas stood before the mirror that hung near the front door. She gazed at her reflection. She was small and slender. Her royal blue dress was tucked tight around her tiny waist. Her black hair, shining and straight, hung down her back, but was trimmed short on the sides and over her forehead, in the fashion of unmarried Algonquin maidens. Her dark eyes in her deep-golden face were like the eyes of a doe.

Just then she was startled by a loud knock at the front door.

She heard Mrs. Whitaker call from the back, "You may see who it is, Pocahontas."

She lifted the doorlatch and opened the door.

A tall man stood there. Seeing her, he smiled and took off his black English hat. His hair was brown and streaked with gold. His skin looked nearly as golden as her own. He clearly spent much time in the sun. His clear gray eyes looked kind and honest.

"My name is John Rolfe," he said. "You must be the Princess Pocahontas, and I'm very honored to meet you." He bowed, then stood silently. She knew he was waiting for her to respond, but her mind was blank. What was it she should say?

"Pocahontas, I've heard about your wisdom and knowledge," he finally went on, "and I've come from Jamestown to seek your advice. I want to know the best ways of growing crops in this land. I know you and your people have discovered so much about—"

"Pocahontas!" It was Mrs. Whitaker's voice behind her. Pocahontas whirled around.

"Pocahontas, my child," Mrs. Whitaker said, "won't you ask Mr. Rolfe to come in?"

Now Pocahontas remembered the right thing to say to a guest at the door.

"Oh, but it's quite all right, Mrs. Whitaker," Mr. Rolfe quickly put in. "I was just asking the Princess if I could escort her for a short walk in the garden and fields nearby, so I could ask her questions about raising better crops."

"I'm sure the Princess would be pleased," Mrs. Whitaker said. She took a soft shawl from a peg by the door, and draped it around Pocahontas's shoulders. Mr. Rolfe held his arm toward her, and Pocahontas slipped her hand in the crook of his elbow.

As they walked away toward the fields, she looked back and saw Mrs. Whitaker watching with a smile.

They spent the rest of the afternoon together in the fields and the forest. Pocahontas quickly regained her ability to speak, and gave answers to all his questions. Talking with Mr. Rolfe she realized again how much she knew about everything that grew around the Chesapeake. She was thankful again for all that Powhatan and the Brothers had taught her.

She also had questions for Mr. Rolfe. "What is the reason for the English fashion that makes dresses come out so far?" she asked.

"There is no reason," Mr. Rolfe answered. "It's a stupid fashion." They laughed together.

She mentioned seeing a few English men who had hats with strange feathers in them.

"Oh, yes," he said, "ostrich feathers."

"What is this bird ostrich? What does it look like?"

With a stick in the dirt he drew a picture.

She asked, "Is it that you cannot draw well, or does the ostrich really look so strange?"

"Both," he answered, and they laughed again.

He shared funny stories with her from his childhood. He told how he once hid a small fox in his room to save it from the hunting hounds, and how it scared his mother into a faint when she found it.

Pocahontas told him about Little Otter.

Then she asked why John Rolfe had come to this land so far from England. He answered that he believed God wanted him here. He told her he first came across the ocean with his wife and newborn son, but they were killed when the ship was wrecked by a storm. Even through that great sadness, he said, he had not lost his faith in God.

He showed her the small Bible he always carried in his pocket, and a little book he called a Prayer Book. But now the afternoon was over. Since she was learning to read, he promised to let her read from the Prayer Book when he returned to Henrico.

As the summer days eased into fall, another Bearded One came into her life. He was a Spaniard, the first Spaniard Pocahontas had ever met. He said his ship had been wrecked in the Chesapeake in a storm. Of all the Spanish crew, only he had survived. The English found him wandering near Jamestown. The Governor asked the Whitakers to let him stay for a while in their large house.

His name was Don Pablo, and Pocahontas did not like him. His eyes always followed every move that she and the Whitakers made. Pocahontas wondered if he was a spy.

One evening Reverend Whitaker was discussing a Bible story with Pocahontas and patiently answering her questions. Don Pablo was sitting in a corner of the room, listening. He blurted out, "You Englishmen are so strange! You spend such time and trouble making someone a Christian. Why, we Spaniards would have baptized that girl weeks ago!"

"I want to be sure she understands," Reverend Whitaker answered politely. "I want her to make her choice freely and on her own."

John Rolfe returned often to Henrico, and each time Pocahontas enjoyed walking and talking with him. One cool and cloudy afternoon she was reading aloud from his Prayer Book. She paused after she read the sentence, "We renounce the devil and his works."

"Pocahontas, do you understand those words?" Mr. Rolfe asked. She saw the north wind tossing his golden-brown hair.

"Oh, yes!" Pocahontas answered. "I think I understand them better than any English do."

His eyes showed surprise.

Pocahontas continued, "I think I've seen the devil and his works in ways you haven't." She had never spoken to any white man about the Dark Magic and the blood sacrifices that Okewas demanded. But now with many tears she poured out to John Rolfe everything she had seen and heard. She told how she still missed her childhood friend, Lominas-who-was-no-more.

When she came to the end of the long story, she said, "And there is something else that I think I understand and love better than the English do. It's the truth that Jesus died on the cross so we ourselves don't have to make any blood sacrifices." John Rolfe nodded. He told her that his ancestors across the ocean had also been guilty of child-sacrifice in the days before they learned about Jesus.

"Now I know," Pocahontas continued, "that Jesus is the perfect blood-sacrifice, and the only true sacrifice. So the devil Okewas has no right to demand anything from us."

After their talk that day, Pocahontas walked back into the house and found Reverend Whitaker seated at his writing table. "Sir, do you believe I'm ready to be baptized as a Christian?" she asked.

He stood and wrapped her in his arms. "Yes, my child," he answered. "You're ready."

CHAPTER SEVENTEEN

OPEN DOOR

ON A COLD SUNDAY MORNING in the time of year which the English call February, Pocahontas was baptized in the church at Jamestown. She also took another name, a Christian name. She chose to be called Rebecca. The Bible story of Rebecca was one of her favorites. Rebecca in the Bible was brave, and she traveled far to find both her husband and her faith in God.

John Rolfe and the Whitakers stood by her side the day she was baptized. The following week, Mr. Rolfe came again to Henrico for a walk with Pocahontas.

"I've been wondering," he asked her. "What will your people think if you go back to them as a Christian? What will happen to you?"

"I hope I can still become the Spirit Woman of a village, as my father intended. I can show the people the true things I have learned about God's Spirit, and about his Son."

"But can you stand alone against all the Spirit Men who serve Okewas? Won't you be in danger?"

"I don't know," she said softly.

They stopped walking and faced each other. He wrapped

her hands in his. "What if you don't go back?" he said. "What if you stay here forever — with me?"

Pocahontas could find no words to answer.

He took a folded sheet of paper from his pocket, and said, "Let me read what I've written about you in a letter to the Governor: 'My best thoughts and my best hopes are about Pocahontas, and with your wise permission, Governor, I would seek her hand in marriage. She has shown herself so strong in her faith. I believe that God, who never fails us, has opened this door, both for her happiness and for mine.' "

He folded up the letter and put it back in his pocket. "Pocahontas, I would not have written these words if I didn't believe that you care as much for me as I care for you."

Finally she was able to speak. "It is true. I care for you very much."

He got down on his knees before her, something Pocahontas had never seen any man do before a woman.

His voice was a gentle whisper. "Then, my dear, will you become my wife?"

Pocahontas got down on her knees, too. "Yes, John Rolfe, I will."

Several weeks later, on the fifth day of the time of year which the English call April, a day of celebration was proclaimed for everyone in the land of the Chesapeake. It was the wedding day of Princess Rebecca Matoaka Pocahontas, the daughter of Powhatan, great King of All the Chesapeake.

Old Chief Powhatan did not come to the church in Jamestown for the ceremony. But he gave his blessing to the marriage, and sent his daughter a necklace of perfectly matched pearls for a wedding gift. He sent Parahunt to stand in his place to give the hand of Pocahontas to the Englishman John Rolfe. Parahunt wore leather breeches and a vest with white fringe.

Standing in a ring of celebration around the church were one hundred and fifty braves, all fully painted and wearing their proudest feather headdresses.

Pocahontas wore the pearls from Powhatan, and a headband made by Halewa, and a lacy white dress made by Mrs. Whitaker. She carried wildflowers that she picked herself that morning.

A feast followed the ceremony. Algonquin and English sat together and ate the best foods from the sea and the forest and the fields. Then a prancing black horse pulled a cart that carried the newly married couple to a house on a nearby hill. It was the house John Rolfe had built for his bride.

A new time of peace between the Algonquins and the English had begun.

A year later, on another spring day, Pocahontas was wearing her buckskin dress and was walking along a forest trail. Bundled on her back was her new baby, Thomas. They were going to visit the child's grandfather, whom Pocahontas herself had not seen for nearly six years.

When they reached the village of Rassa-wack, Pocahontas carefully took the bundle off her back, and pulled aside the fur and deerskin wrappings from little Thomas. She held the child in her arms, and walked into the council longhouse.

She was prepared to be surprised at how old her father looked. Still, the sight of his deeply lined face brought a mist of sadness to her eyes.

Seated on his fur-covered throne, Powhatan held out his arms. She handed him the child, and Powhatan hugged him to his chest.

"This baby is beautiful," the great chief announced. "A perfect baby. And he must have a royal name. I shall call him Pepsi-canow — Mighty Waters."

Pocahontas stepped forward and kneeled. She put her head on her father's knee. She felt his hand stroking her hair.

When she looked up at him, he opened his heart to talk with her, as he had done in the days so long ago.

"Is this good, my child — this mixing of English blood with Algonquin blood? Is it not like the meeting of two kinds of waters, the salt of the ocean and the fresh water of the river?"

She answered with gentleness. "No, my father, it is more like the meeting of two great rivers that join together into a new one. And the river-of-their-joining is far greater and more powerful."

She wasn't far from Rassa-wack on her journey home when Pocahontas heard a loud rustle on the thick wooded hillside sloping up from the trail. She stopped and peered through the trees. It hadn't sounded like an animal's noise.

Her first thought made her shiver with fear: She remembered the old Spirit Man and his two priests waving hatchets on the day they came after the three boys near Comoco. That was the last time she had seen the Quiyow. She was a new and stronger person now because of her faith in Jesus, but still she hoped desperately that she would not have to face that Spirit Man again.

There was silence now on the hillside, and she saw nothing through the trees. She reached behind her to make sure the bundle with Baby Thomas was strapped on as tightly as possible. Then she turned and walked steadily along the trail, without looking back.

CHAPTER EIGHTEEN

ROYAL GOODBYE

ANOTHER YEAR went by, and the peace between Algonquin and English continued. Already it was being called "The Peace of Pocahontas."

Then came a spring day when Pocahontas and John were standing on the busy dock at Jamestown. Out in the river was a three-masted ship, the *Treasurer*, bound for England. One-year-old Thomas stood between his parents on wobbly legs, clinging to his mother's dress.

They were part of a group of Algonquins and English from the land of the Chesapeake who had been invited to England by important people there. Most of the rest of the travelers had already boarded the ship — including Remcoe and Kahnessa, and old friend Percy, and the Governor, and even Captain Argall.

Powhatan was sending along Tomo-como, one of his chief warriors at Rassa-wack. Tomo-como was leaning on a stick at the edge of the dock. It was a counting stick. Powhatan had instructed him to put a notch in the stick for every ten men he saw after the ship arrived in London. That way he could bring back to Powhatan a trustworthy report of the number of people living in England.

Pocahontas wished Tomo-como was not going. He was a strong worshiper of Okewas. Even today he was fully painted in black, and he wore a gray wolfskin on his back. The head of the wolf crowned his hair. He even had live garter snakes in his ears.

Suddenly Pocahontas caught her breath in fear. Walking onto the dock behind Tomo-como was the old Quiyow.

He walked straight to Pocahontas. He stood, and turned all his evil concentration upon her.

"I have come to curse your journey," he snarled. "The power of Okewas will drag this ship to the bottom of the Great Gray Ocean. I promise you, Matoaka, that you will never reach the land of the Tassen-tassees."

John Rolfe tightened his arms around Pocahontas. She knew he did not understand the Spirit Man's Algonquin words, but he must have guessed their meaning. Baby Thomas started crying, and Pocahontas reached down to sweep him into her arms.

The Quiyow chanted and hissed, then went away.

"Don't be afraid, Pocahontas," John told her, as he contin-ued his embrace. "God is with you, and with me, and with little Thomas. We're in his hands, and he is far mightier than the evil one."

Moments later they were on board the ship. Pocahontas found courage in her husband's strength. She let the memory of the Quiyow slip from her mind, and she let her faith in God be strong.

"We're in his hands," she repeated to herself.

The breeze grew stronger. Above her she saw the great white

sails roll down and fill with wind. She thought again of giant swans.

"Heave away!" the men who worked the ship were shouting. "Cast off!"

The *Treasurer* rolled away from Jamestown. In just moments they were racing before the wind. Their speed took her breath away, as Pocahontas stood by the rail, clinging to John and Thomas.

Soon they were rounding a tip of land that would hide their view of Jamestown. The ship began splitting the waves of the Chesapeake, the great bay that carried all the riverwaters of this land out to sea.

There before them, Pocahontas saw an awesome sight.

Coming down from the north was a great long dugout with forty paddlers — Powhatan's royal barge! Around it were many smaller canoes. All the Algonquins in all the boats were in full ceremonial feathers and paint.

Over the sun-sparkled waves came the sound of the tribal paddling song, and the beat of tom-toms.

Mighty Powhatan stood in the rear of his longboat, his feet planted wide. High above his head he slowly waved a staff of eagle feathers, a royal goodbye to his royal daughter.

All the *Treasurer's* passengers ran to the side of the ship to stand by Pocahontas and enjoy this gathered greeting.

Pocahontas kept waving back, and she never took her eyes from her father's boat. Soon it became only a sliver on the horizon, and still she saw his uplifted staff waving, waving. Finally, it was gone from sight.

The Princess gave one last wave in return.

With the first light of the next morning, Pocahontas hurried on deck to feel again the salt spray in her face, and the force of the sea wind. Soon John joined her at the railing. They saw whales surfacing not far away. Pocahontas told John how her brothers had always hunted the mighty whales.

"And since you were always adventurous," John said, "did you want to go with them?"

"I knew the whale hunts were too dangerous," she answered. "But once I hid in Parahunt's canoe and tried to go with him on his first trip to spy on Jamestown. But they caught me first, and took me back home. I thought I might never get to go on an adventure in my life. And now, look where I am!"

Five weeks later Pocahontas was in her cabin below deck on the *Treasurer*, rocking baby Thomas. She heard the ship's bell ring, and a shout, "Land, ho!"

Footsteps pounded as the passengers rushed from their cabins. Pocahontas wrapped her son in a blanket and followed them on deck. John was there, and greeted her with an excited smile. He pulled her to the rail and pointed to a gray line on the horizon. England was in sight.

"The captain says this is his shortest crossing ever," John told her.

Tono-como was standing nearby. The snakes in his ears had not survived the crossing. Pocahontas watched as he pulled the dead, withered reptiles from his ears, and threw them over the rail. They floated away on the waves, left behind by the speeding ship.

EPILOGUE

THE *TREASURER* made it to England in the late spring of the year 1616. Tomo-como abandoned his counting stick soon after he first laid eyes on London's crowded streets.

Princess Pocahontas — also known as Lady Rebecca Rolfe — was introduced to many of the most famous people of her day in England. She saw a play by William Shakespeare in the Globe Theatre. She spent a day in Parliament.

She was also presented before Queen Anne, the wife of King James. When Pocahontas curtseyed, the queen stood and bowed her head in return. "We are both of royal blood, my child," the queen said. Pocahontas later met King James as well.

John Smith was still alive, Pocahontas discovered. He had written a letter to Queen Anne, and in it he told how Pocahontas had saved his life and the lives of others in Jamestown. "Without her," he wrote, "all was surely lost." He reminded the Queen that Pocahontas was "the first of her great Nation to become a Christian." Pocahontas was later able to meet with Captain Smith. She learned that he had always hoped to return to the Chesapeake.

After several months in England, Pocahontas and her family made their plans to return home. But Pocahontas had become ill, and her sickness grew worse. She died in March of 1617, at the age of twenty, and her body was buried in England.

When John Smith learned of her death, he wrote these words in a letter: "When we think of all the young Princess accomplished, not only for my sake, but for her people and for all she cared for in Jamestown, we can only say one thing: Surely it was God who made Pocahontas."

HISTORICAL NOTE

THE RECORDS OF HISTORY paint for us this picture of the true Pocahontas: She was born in 1597 in Chief Powhatan's village of Werowocomoco (in this book we call it "Comoco" for short). We know that she was only about ten years old when she stopped her people from putting to death the English Captain John Smith. We also know that later the English colonists in Jamestown often saw her turning cartwheels when she visited there. She was lovely and small and quick.

We know a great deal about her father, Powhatan, and his large family. Pocahontas was his favorite daughter. Tatacoope and Parahunt were the real names of two of her many brothers. We also know about some of her sisters.

The people worshiped the War God Okewas. We know that the old Quiyoughcosuck (the Quiyow in this book), the priest of the Okewas, wore live-snake earrings, and that he and Pocahontas were in conflict. We know that human sacrifices to Okewas numbered in the hundreds.

Pocahontas was present in Jamestown when Ratcliffe falsely accused Captain Smith, and when Newport's ship arrived from England. We know the names of some of the men whom Pocahontas warned on the "night of terror" portrayed in this book, and we know the names of three English boys whose rescue she attempted from Werowocomoco.

From many letters and diaries we know much about her time in Henrico with Reverend and Mrs. Whitaker, her romance and marriage to John Rolfe, and the birth of their son Thomas. Even the Spaniard at Henrico was a real person, a spy for the Spanish. In his letters to his king he wrote, "The English parson is very slow in his dealings with the Indian Princess, making sure that her faith is her own — how unlike we Spanish who would have baptized her long ago!"

We also know a great deal about her days in England — even the balls she attended and the homes in which she was a guest. She met the poet and playwright Ben Jonson and the explorer Walter Raleigh. We know that she greatly impressed the English royal family.

We also know of the "great confession of her faith" which she gave as she lay dying in the town of Gravesend, England. Her dying words were that she had great assurance of the resurrection. She also said she wanted her young son Thomas to be raised by his father's parents in England, so he could return one day to the Chesapeake as a well-learned man of faith and be a blessing to both the Algonquins and the English.

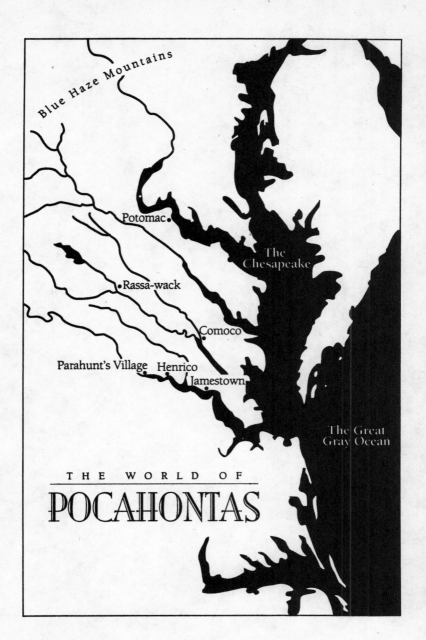

Blue Haze Mountains

Potomac

The Chesapeake

Rassa-wack

Comoco

Parahunt's Village

Henrico

Jamestown

The Great
Gray Ocean

THE WORLD OF

POCAHONTAS